Kagoshima

Tokyo

Osaka

NANBAN AT THE WELL

195 St John Street, Clerkenwell, London EC1V 4JY

なんばん

Special dishes from KAGOSHIMA PREFECTURE

juice

Satsuma Sour 薩摩サワー
Shochu with satsuma-yuzu sour mix

hips

Tuna Tataki 鰹たたき
Seared tuna served with ginger, real wasabi, and orange ponzu dip

Kagoshima Ramen 鹿児島ラーメン
Thin noodles in a dashi-pork broth blend with pork belly, burnt garlic oil, tea-pickled egg, fried shallots, pickled daikon, etc.

ty

Yaki Imo 焼き芋
Baked sweet potato with yuzu butter

eese

Shirokuma しろくま
Shaved ice with condensed milk, sweet black beans, and fresh fruit

te

Organic Matcha from Kagoshima
鹿児島産オーガニック抹茶

How to eat ramen

Grab a mouthful of noodles and toppings with your chopsticks and slurp with great vigour to hoover up broth along with the solid ingredients. Pro tip: make a lot of noise. Use the spoon as needed to scoop up more broth and feel free to drink the broth directly from the bowl.

Special thanks to Mizore for [...] use of their shave ice machine and to Lalani & Co. for suppl[...] their excellent tea.

NANBAN at PACIFIC SOCIAL CLUB

Special Dishes from Kumamoto Prefecture

2 November, 2013

Karashi Renkon
辛子レンコン
Lotus root stuffed with hot mustard-miso paste

Takana Meshi
高菜飯
Rice cooked with spicy fermented mustard greens

Maitake Mushroom Miso Soup
舞茸のみそ汁
Maitake dashi with miso, maitake, pearl barley, and spring onions

Horse Katsu
桜肉カツ
Horse rump, breaded and deep-fried, served with umeboshi slaw and katsu sauce

...to Orange Cheesecake
オレンジのチーズケーキ
...nge and ricotta cake with [...] to puree and a kinako crust

Kumamoto is here, in the centre of Kyushu. It is famous for volcanoes, horse sashimi, citrus fruits, and its majestic castle, among other things.

This is Kumamon, the official mascot of Kumamoto prefecture. He is one of the most popular characters in Japan. Recently, his trademark red cheeks were stolen by a scoundrel.

Hitomoji Guru-guru
一文字ぐるぐる
Blanched spring onions, wrapped into bundles and served with a sweet miso dip

Iwashi Mentai
鰯めんたい
Grilled sardines stuffed with mentaiko (chilli-cured cod roe)

Rafutē
ラフテー
Pork belly braised in soy sauce, brown sugar, and awamori (Okinawan rice liquor)

Mini Nagasaki Chanpon
ミニ長崎チャンポン
Noodles in blended chicken and pork broth topped with stir-fried shellfish, cabbage, bean sprouts, bacon, and pickled ginger

Yuzu-Koshō Chicken Yaki-Onigiri
柚子胡椒地鶏炭火焼の焼きおにぎり
Grilled rice balls filled with grilled chicken in a spicy yuzu marinade

Mojiko Roll Cake
門司港ロールケーキ
Black sesame sponge, banana custard, fresh fruit, and green tea whipped cream

On the right is a map of **Kyushu**, Japan's southernmost major island. The arrows point to where each dish originates.

ETM GROUP

MIZORE

LALANI & CO LONDON
EARTH'S MOST PRECIOUS LEAVES

なんばん
NANBAN

なんばん

NANBAN at THE PRINCE ARTHUR
26 & 27 March, 2013

NANBANとDOYAとSHOFOODOH
(Tim Anderson) (Patrick Knill) (Fumio Tanga)
は BREWDOG SHOREDITCH で
P R E S E N T

旨馬

UMA UMA*

* (tasty horse)

In many areas of Japan horse meat is **considered a delicacy,** and we've often wondered how British people would react to horse dishes on a Japanese menu. The recent horse meat scandal is disturbing for many reasons, but also revelatory; while most people (naturally) object to unwittingly eating horse when it's labelled otherwise, they aren't necessarily averse to eating it in general. This surprised us, and encouraged us to get together and create a tasting menu featuring horse. These are mostly classic dishes from around Japan, with a few of our own twists, plus a welcome cocktail and drinks to accompany each course.

SIX DISHES と SEVEN DRINKS

Monday,
18日3月2013年
arrive 19:00
for 19:30 start

@ BrewDog Shoreditch
51-55 Bethnal Green Road • E1 6LA

Horse Menchi Katsu
panko-crusted horse mince cutlet, tartar sauce

Horse Yukhoe
Korean/Kumamoto-style tenderloin tartare, shiso, sesame toast

Miyazaki Nadōfu
freshly made tofu set with bits of veg, sweet miso dressing

Horse Okonomiyaki
Hiroshima-style savory pancake with cabbage, horse meat, okonomi sauce, spring onions, etc.

Uma-don
thinly sliced horse, sweet soy sauce, onions, rice

Baniwa Ice
horse hair, pony snaps, barnyard sorbet

Unfortunately we can make no menu substitutions to accommodate special dietary requirements for this event.

NANBAN WHIPPY-SAN* SOCIAL
AT THE EUSTON CIDER TAP

なんばんのこだわり日本風味ソフトクリーム新発売/[...]

* Whippy-san is what we call Japanese Mr. [...]
In Japan, it's usually called soft cream, short for 'soft serve[...]
But whatever you call it, it's delicious. Light, sweet, and creamy[...]
Whippy we know and love, in delightful and exotic Japanese[...]

Saturday, 9 March | Sunday, 10 [...]

SATSUMA VANILLA
(バニラみかん)

RAMUNE
(ラムネ • Japanese Lemonade)

SAKU[...]
(桜 • Cherry Blosso[...])

MISO CARAM[...]
(味噌キャラメル)

We'll be serving from around 14:00 on each day, starting with the firs[...]
selling that until it runs out. Then we'll move onto the next flavour. (U[...]
it costs twice as much to hire a machine that dispenses two flavours at [...]
also be offering cider floats and specially selected apple brandies to pe[...]
Whippy-san!

Satsuma Spice Tonpī
みかんスパイスのトンピー
Pork crackling with satsuma zest, chilli powder, and salt

Brussels Sprouts Champloo
芽キャベツのチャンプルー
Stir-fried Brussels sprouts, tofu, egg, and ham

Winter Warmer Rafutē
クリスマス酒の味ラフテー
Pork belly simmered in soy sauce, Christmas ale, and port

Ox Cheek Taco Rice
牛のほほ肉タコライス
Braised ox cheek with a pinch of mixed spice, grated cheddar, kimchi rice, and burnt lettuce

D1604477

Nanban

なんばん

For Japanophiles
everywhere

Nanban
なんばん

JAPANESE
SOUL FOOD

Tim Anderson

CLARKSON POTTER/PUBLISHERS

NEW YORK

Contents
目次

Introduction
The Story of Nanban

It all started in Wisconsin

Like any other state, Wisconsin has its own unique gastronomy. But when I was growing up, it didn't feel very unique. My state's local specialties—mostly of distant Germanic origin—never seemed all that local, or all that special. What I ate as a kid and a teenager seemed exactly like my hometown: boring, broad and generic.

Which is not to say I didn't like it. I always did enjoy macaroni and cheese, bratwurst, Danish pastries and sauerkraut. That's good eatin'. Now that I'm an old man, I get nostalgic for stuff like that. But back then I was restless. I knew there was more out there, and I wanted to taste it.

I knew there was more because when I was 14, I got hooked on a Japanese TV show called *Iron Chef*, wherein elite chefs challenged the even more elite "Iron Chefs" to 60-minute cookery battles centered on a secret theme ingredient. These ingredients ranged from the mundane (milk) to the luxurious (lobster) to the unheard of (*konnyaku*—WTF?).

The show was regularly ridiculed by the mass media, as it was by my friends and family. To be fair, there was a lot to make fun of. The host (or "chairman," as he was officially known) dressed and behaved kind of like a Japanese Liberace. The commentary was dubbed in awkwardly translated English, like an old kung fu movie. And the dishes that the chefs produced were frequently outlandish, at least by Middle American standards. I recall a number of seafood-based ice creams, which nowadays have become passé thanks to countless Adrià and Blumenthal imitators (myself included). But back in 1999 in Wisconsin, sea urchin gelato seemed positively insane. An *Iron Chef* parody on *Saturday Night Live* featured "eel farts," which goes to show just how bizarre many viewers found some of the food.

Nobody in Wisconsin had ever seen anything like it, and I was enthralled. I remember watching with wide-eyed horror as an Iron Chef cut the head off an enormous live octopus as it flailed and grappled for its life. I swooned over the cute and talented Kumiko Kobayashi, a rare female challenger in the high-tension Mishima beef battle. I learned about "cheffy" ingredients like foie gras, swallow's nest and caviar. It was entertainment first and foremost, but it was also an education. Or at least the start of one.

Iron Chef appeared around the same time that I started to discover other aspects of Japanese pop culture: Nintendo, J-pop and anime. One day, as my friend Justin and I perused videos and video games at the mall, he matter-of-factly proclaimed, "Japanese stuff is cool." That simple truth instantly lodged itself in my brain. I developed a love for all manner of things Japanese, with a particular passion for Japanese cuisine. I was enamored with it—or at least I tried hard to be. Truth be told, I didn't love sushi at first. I thought the textures were weird, I didn't fancy the flavor of seaweed and I found much of it pretty bland.

I made frequent sushi-eating trips to Milwaukee and Chicago in attempts to acquire a taste for it. It's an odd thing, to work really hard at making yourself like something, and I don't think it's something many people do. But it would have been incongruous, and weird, to like Japanese food in theory but not in practice. So I soldiered on, stuffing my big American face with dainty pieces of raw tuna, deep-fried shrimp and fake crab.

Ultimately, of course, I did acquire a taste for sushi, and by the time I graduated from high school, I had a basic working knowledge of Japanese food. That knowledge developed further on my first vacation to Japan, which came as a graduation present from my parents in the summer of 2002. I was accompanied by my dad and my oldest friend—Justin, the same one who had planted the Japanophilia seed in my fertile brain.

I wish I could say that I loved every mouthful of food I tried, but in reality I was totally inexperienced with authentic Japanese cuisine, so I found some of the flavors and textures off-putting. I recall buying a bottle of green tea that tasted so briny I was convinced it was brewed with seaweed, and my first sashimi dinner was a chewy struggle. But I fell in love with Japan—it surpassed my greatest expectations—and I remained excited and intrigued by its food, even if I hadn't quite gone native in terms of my tastes.

Of course, there were certain dishes I'd come to love unconditionally, like fried rice, *gyoza* and just about anything grilled on a stick. By age 18, my enthusiasm for Japanese food was as much a part of my personality as anything. But when you're in Wisconsin, you can only really scratch the surface of Japanese gastronomy. There just isn't much there. Largely for that reason—and also because I knew I was way too cool for my stupid, boring podunk hometown—I decided to go to college in California, America's gateway to Japan.

In California, they serve sushi in little boats

That's what I discovered while visiting colleges in Los Angeles, a metropolis so saturated with sushi joints that many of them resort to silly gimmicks. At the awkwardly punctuated A'Float Sushi in Pasadena, it's the parade of wooden serving boats that circumnavigate the sushi bar through a tiny canal—a playful twist on the standard *kaiten-zushi* (conveyor-belt sushi) format.

I was enrolled at Occidental College, a small school in northeastern LA, in the fall of 2002. One of the first things I did once I moved in was bum a ride to Little Tokyo. When I got there I completely geeked out—particularly in the Japanese supermarkets. I think I may have even jumped up and down with excitement. I had dabbled in the kitchen as a teenager (I took great pride in my egg salad sandwiches), but for the most part, I didn't cook when I was a student. I lived in dorms and ate in dining halls, so when I went to Japanese grocery stores my purchases tended toward junk food and snacks: green tea sweets, *mochi* (rice cakes), instant noodles and potato chips with exotic flavors like chicken ramen and *nori* seaweed. I certainly wasn't sampling the heights of Japanese gastronomy, but at the very least, I was introducing myself to flavors and foods common in Japanese culinary pop culture. And isn't that the most important kind of culture?

Maybe it isn't. But I was a student, and I didn't have the money to eat out at nice places, and at any rate, I had little interest in them. In a city where I could get some of the best tacos on the planet for $1.50 apiece, it seemed pointless to shell out $30 on a high-end sushi dinner. When I did go out for Japanese, it tended to be humbler, more affordable fare: noodles, rice bowls, pork cutlets and the like. Besides, although I had come to love sushi, it still wasn't one of my favorite Japanese dishes. Like many people, I'd entered the world of Japanese food through the sushi bar. But that led to new and unexpected delights, like the savory cabbage pancake called *okonomiyaki*, the fine buckwheat noodles known as *soba* and mild yet satisfying Japanese curry.

And then there was ramen

I can't quite remember how and when I first learned about *ramen*. I think it was one of those things that trickled in to my consciousness from various sources: fellow Japanophiles, friends who had studied in Japan and just the sheer ubiquity of ramen shops in LA's Little Tokyo. It was something I knew was important to modern Japanese cuisine, but I wasn't sure exactly why.

My first few ramen experiences failed to impress. I'd wandered into a few shops, ordered their most basic bowl, slurped, shrugged and went on my way. But in 2004, on an unusually dreary LA autumn night, I was out in Little Tokyo with my then-girlfriend and a too-large group of friends. Nowhere could accommodate the eight of us. After a half hour of fruitless wandering, we came across an unassuming ramen shop called Daikokuya, which took us in.

I have had only a handful of food revelations in my life, and this was one of them. The broth was preternaturally piggy and rich; the noodles were bouncy and full of verve; the pork belly was throbbing with flavor yet cooked to this incredible melt-in-the-mouth softness, on the brink of complete disintegration. And then there were the toppings and condiments to bring contrast, complexity and balance: musky minced garlic, crunchy bamboo shoots and bean sprouts, nutty sesame seeds, sharp pickled ginger, fresh scallions and a marinated boiled egg, its yolk cooked until set but still creamy. It was a deceptively complex and utterly mesmerizing bowl of food.

At last, I knew what all the fuss was about. This was the real deal. I became a regular at Daikokuya, eating there fortnightly until I graduated two years later. I almost never ordered anything but the ramen.

At this point I was so obsessed with Japanese food that I'd started to shoehorn it into my education, and in 2005, my Japanese language professor nominated me for a research grant. I proposed an ambitious project to study various noodle cultures in Japan (soba, udon and ramen) in historical, social and regional contexts. (Nerd alert!) I got the grant and set off on a four-week tour of some of Japan's noodliest destinations. That may sound like a lazy academic luxury, and in many ways it was, but the grant was only $3,000—and that had to cover the airfare and internal train travel as well as accommodations. In Kyoto I stayed at a hostel called Kyoto Cheapest Inn. It cost ¥900 a night (about $10), and I had to sleep on the floor with no pillow. Those were the days!

If I'm honest, I wasn't enormously diligent in my research. Mainly I ate noodles and drank Japanese alcopops called chu-hi (more on those later). But I did learn quite a lot, and after a week or so I decided to refocus my thesis on the peculiar phenomenon of food museums, one of which is the inimitable Ramen Museum in Yokohama. Less a real museum than a vaguely educational food court/theme park, it houses eight different ramen shops, each considered one of the country's best. To have an outpost in the Ramen Museum is an honor; it's like the Rock and Roll Hall of Fame, but for noodles.

To provide proper context, the ramen shops are situated in a meticulously detailed re-creation of a generic Japanese downtown circa 1958 (the year instant ramen was invented), complete with fake bars and pachinko parlors, old movie billboards and a surprisingly convincing perpetual sunset. All of this is meant to evoke a sense of nostalgia to accompany your food—and it is a powerful framing device, even for those of us who didn't live in Japan in the fifties. Rice is often thought of as Japan's national food, but the museum makes a strong argument that it's actually ramen. Its endless adaptability and status as vaguely foreign (it's originally Chinese) have made it a dish without a centralized tradition but a huge place in the collective consciousness. In ramen, variation is the norm rather than the exception, so every region of Japan has its own homegrown style. And I gleaned that Kyushu (pronounced "Q-shoe"), the southernmost major island of the Japanese archipelago, is perhaps the most celebrated ramen region.

So I knew I had to go to Kyushu

I had wanted to live in Japan since high school, so in my senior year of college I applied to the Japanese Exchange and Teaching (JET) Program, a government initiative to bring native English speakers to Japan to teach. On the application form, they ask you for three places you'd like to live. I chose all of mine based on their ramen: Yokohama, Sapporo and Fukuoka. To my delight, I got Fukuoka.

More specifically, I was placed in Kitakyushu ("North Kyushu"), a city of 1 million, overshadowed by neighboring Fukuoka's 1.3 million. When I got there, I must admit it was not love at first sight. Kitakyushu is an old manufacturing town—during World War II, it was a major site of military production, and it was only spared the A-bomb due to cloud cover on the day it was scheduled to drop. (The Americans bombed nearby Nagasaki instead.) Kitakyushu's manufacturing industry isn't as dominant as it was back then, but a haze of beige smog still hangs in the air, and the city has a ramshackle and rusty look about it. But of course, I wasn't there to drink in the sights. I was there to eat. And the food did not disappoint. Good ramen was everywhere, and beyond that, the local cuisine was incredibly idiosyncratic and diverse.

I started eating my way around Fukuoka prefecture, trying things like motsu nabe (offal hot pot, pages 108–109), kashiwa-meshi (chicken rice) and karashi mentaiko (chili-cured pollock roe, pages 50–51). In many ways, it was like encountering Japanese food for the first time again—there were so many things I'd never seen before, and so many tastes to acquire! Mentaiko in particular weirded me out—fish eggs in their sacs, flaccid and pink, aren't the most appetizing thing in the world upon first glance. But they have inner beauty.

From Fukuoka I started exploring the rest of Kyushu. I briefly dated a girl in nearby Saga prefecture, famous for rice and crab dishes. When she dumped me, I went on a weekend away to collect myself in Kumamoto, where I sampled hot mustard–stuffed lotus root (pages 74–75), horsemeat sashimi (pages 76–77) and extraordinarily addictive Kumamoto ramen, characterized by chips of fried garlic (pages 176–177). Then there were excursions to Nagasaki, with its Chinese-inflected specialties like steamed pork buns; Kagoshima, the sweet-potato capital of Japan; and Miyazaki, a subtropical paradise of citrus fruit, mangoes and free-range chicken. Toward the end of my tenure I also spent a day in Oita, so I could boast that I had been to every prefecture in Kyushu. And I fell in love with them all.

I also fell in love with an English girl named Laura. We were working together in the same city, and after one fateful, drunken karaoke session, I missed the last train home and had to crash at her tiny apartment. One thing led to another, and here we are, seven years later, happily married and living in London.

Though I was and always will be a Japanophile, when I moved to the UK, I knew I had to put my love for things Japanese out of mind if I was going to thrive. London has a charm all its own, but it is not Los Angeles or Fukuoka—at that time, the Japanese food scene in the Big Smoke was rudimentary and mostly split into two camps: terrible high-street convenience food or over-designed, style-conscious eateries made by and for people with too much money.

I found a lot to love about British food and drink—especially real ale and the mighty pile of food called a ploughman's lunch. But still, I dreamt of ramen, and I dreamt of Kyushu. But it wasn't a dream to go back—it was a dream to bring them here. Where were the *tonkotsu* ramen shops, I wondered? Where was the *yaki-curry* (pages 90–91) and the *karashi renkon* (pages 74–75)? They would be such a hit with the British people, I thought. I loved the idea of opening a restaurant—and the name Nanban came easily—but I had no idea where to start. It was a pipe dream, but a persistent one. I couldn't get it out of my head.

I applied to MasterChef

I did it on a whim, egged on by Laura. It took about 20 minutes to fill out the online application, and then I forgot about it. But about a month down the road, in the

summer of 2010, I got an unexpected phone call—the producers wanted to talk to me. There was then a second interview, in which I had to bring in a cold dish I'd prepared ahead of time. I made a *bento*, a Japanese lunch box, containing eight different things, if memory serves. It was a somewhat strange selection, and none of it was what you might call "traditional": soba noodle salad with tarragon, fried chicken seasoned with green tea, smoked mackerel sushi. I wasn't at all proficient when it came to authentic Japanese cookery, but I was good at exploiting Japanese ingredients to make my food bold and unusual. I think the *MasterChef* auditioners had never tasted anything quite like that weird little bento I brought in.

Later, at the auditions, I made a kind of fish-and-chips with Japanese flavors—or you could just call it cod tempura with sweet potatoes, with a little malt vinegar *ponzu* and pickled ginger tartar sauce on the side. (I still serve the latter with chicken nanban and mackerel Scotch eggs.) I was proud of my tempura skills, but it was a silly dish, and later on judge John Torode told me that if it weren't for my clever and attractive presentation, which included a sheet of Japanese newspaper, I probably wouldn't have gone through.

Weeks later, I found myself battling 19 other hopefuls in an enormous studio kitchen. In the first round we had an invention test. I kept it simple—cod with a new potato and quail's egg salad, salmon roe, crispy shallots, dill, a poached egg and a mustard-cider vinaigrette. It was named one of the best dishes of the day, and apparently also weird enough that judge Gregg Wallace dubbed me the series' "Mad Professor."

If you want to succeed in *MasterChef*—as in most things—you have to have a point of difference. I thought mine would be Japanese (or Japanese-influenced) cookery. But as soon as Gregg called me "Mad Professor," I knew the role I had to play. I never thought I was the best cook in the room. But I figured I could be the most interesting, the one that keeps the judges on their toes, and that might keep me in the running.

Though my cooking on *MasterChef* went in a hyper-modern and wildly ostentatious direction, my one true love, the food that always sprang to mind when people asked what I'd want to eat as a last meal or every day for the rest of my life, remained the same: ramen. Nanban was the *MasterChef* dream, but it wasn't the *MasterChef* strategy. I played the Mad Professor, and it paid off—much to my surprise, I won *MasterChef*, in part due to a souped-up ramen with porcini-infused pork broth and lobster gyoza with black truffles that I served in the final.

The victory afforded me a range of amazing opportunities, from a stage at the Fat Duck to brewing my own limited-edition beer. These experiences were incredible, but they caused me to deviate somewhat from the Nanban path. By 2012, good ramen was already starting to make inroads into London. I had always imagined that I'd be the leader of the ramen revolution, but apparently others had the same idea. The ramen ship had set sail while I was building sandcastles on the shore; in less than a year, London went from having no good ramen shops to speak of to having five.

At first, I found this worrying, but then, encouraging. People were ready for next-level Japanese soul food: "the ramen moment" had arrived. I started to get serious about opening Nanban. After a few months of shopping my business plan around, I found backers and began the long, arduous process of setting up a restaurant: hosting temporary "pop-ups" to test the dishes and drum up interest; hunting for premises; and meeting suppliers, builders and, of course, lawyers.

Alas, it was not to be. After more than a year of struggling to find a site, my backers lost interest in the project and put their money into building chains out of the brands they'd already established. When they walked away, I was pretty distraught—but only briefly. All was not lost! By now, Nanban was established as a successful pop-up *izakaya*—literally, a place to stay and drink (page 216)—and while I'd originally conceived these itinerant events as a prelude to a real restaurant, they'd developed a life and a following of their own.

So I simply kept going, encouraged by the response and support from the customers at my pop-ups. I have been especially happy with the reaction to certain dishes I personally love but wasn't sure the British diners would be on board with: oddities like my yaki-curry (pages 90–91) and *hiyajiru* (cold miso soup, pages 78–79).

The idea for this book came out of this positive reaction, months of recipe development and from the realization that a cookbook is actually a better way of spreading the southern Japanese food gospel than a restaurant. A book—like a pop-up restaurant—can travel, while a bricks-and-mortar restaurant stays in one place. It allows a much broader range of people and home cooks to taste the food I love.

To this end, I've tried to make the recipes as accessible as possible without sacrificing their true flavors. Most of the recipes are very easy to do—the only hurdle may be sourcing some of the ingredients, but with the advent of online shopping, great home-cooked food is now accessible to everyone.

A brief history of Southern Barbarian cuisine

Today, Tokyo is Japan's undisputed center of culture and international exchange and therefore boasts the country's most cosmopolitan cuisine. But for many centuries, this wasn't the case. Kyoto was the political and cultural capital for almost a thousand years, but even then, arguably more interesting and diverse gastronomy was burgeoning elsewhere: at the fringe of the nation, on the southwesternmost island of Kyushu.

Under shogunal rule, interaction with foreign people was tightly restricted, which led to the historical characterization of Edo Japan as an officially "closed country" (*sakoku*). Of course, there were exceptions, perhaps most notably at Nagasaki, on the west coast of Kyushu. Now more tragically known for being razed by an American atomic bomb in World War II, Nagasaki was once renowned as a hub of trade and immigration. Until the mid-19th century it was one of the only cities where exchange with foreigners was permitted, primarily merchants and missionaries from Portugal, the Netherlands, Korea and China, and less commonly, Spain and England. The Dutch even had their own enclave called Dejima, an artificial island protruding into Nagasaki Bay, which still stands as a historic attraction.

The influx of foreign traders into Nagasaki in the 16th and 17th centuries exposed the Japanese to new cooking methods and to ingredients that were, until that time, either taboo (like meat) or prohibitively rare and expensive (like refined sugar). In *Food and Fantasy in Early Modern Japan*, Eric Rath describes a "barbarian cookbook" published in the early 1600s that contains Japanized versions of Portuguese recipes and incorporates many of these new ingredients and techniques. The text shows that Japanese sweets such as Castella (pages 196–197), *marubōlo* (pages 204–205) and the hard candy *konpeitō* were taken directly from the Portuguese, and have changed only slightly in the three or four centuries since they were introduced. Techniques such as deep-frying in batter and cooking with chilies and vinegar also came from the Portuguese, providing the basis for dishes like tempura (pages 96–97) and *nanban-zuke* (pages 104–105). Over time, recipes like these lost their cultural characteristics and connection to their country of origin, and integrated into what would become mainstream Japanese gastronomy (though many still retain a strong association with Nagasaki or Kyushu in general).

In the 19th century, Chinese culinary influence in Nagasaki coincided with a nationwide craze for noodles (mostly soba) and sociopolitical changes that would foster the inception of what is arguably Japan's national dish: ramen. In *Slurp! A Social and Culinary History of Ramen*, Barak Kushner writes:

The men who dominated the Meiji Restoration [a complete political upheaval beginning in 1868] . . . urged for a clean sweep of traditional customs that would pave the way for radical social change, including the development of a meatier diet and the growth of a population becoming gradually more amenable to foreign dishes. . . . Meat, as visitors to the foreign treaty ports noticed, went quite well with noodle dishes, which had already reached high levels of popularity during the Edo period.

By the 1890s, and possibly earlier, Japan had its first ramen, or proto-ramen, on record: a Chinese noodle soup made from pork and vegetable scraps called *chanpon* (pages 178–179) served at a Nagasaki restaurant by an expat chef named Chen Pingjun. Chanpon, in a slightly more refined form, is still a distinctly Nagasaki dish, but ramen in general has spread throughout Japan, fostered by Chinese expat communities producing similar dishes elsewhere.

Japanese cuisine is often thought of as monolithic and impenetrable, but the history of Nagasaki and Kyushu as sites of foreign influences shows that quite the opposite is true: modern Japanese food is made up from a wide mixture of things—not unlike chanpon itself. Just a few centuries ago, dishes like ramen and Castella, which are now considered quintessentially Japanese, would have been thought of as exotic curiosities.

Today, Kyushu remains a center of foreign exchange (Fukuoka is sometimes called the "gateway to Asia"), although now it comes mostly from Korea—hence the popularity of items like karashi mentaiko (pages 50–51) and *namool* (pages 164–165). It is this ongoing and historical influx of other cultures into Kyushu, combined with a strong sense of local pride, that makes southern Japan's food so idiosyncratic. But of course, what is idiosyncratic now will likely become the national norm in a matter of decades—tonkotsu ramen (pages 150–151), for example, has already conquered Japan, and now it's set to conquer the world.

What does "Nanban" mean?

Nanban literally means "southern barbarian," which is what the Japanese originally called Europeans when they first arrived in the south of Japan having traveled via the East Indies. And they were, of course, barbaric. The term is no longer used as an epithet, but it lingers on as a descriptor for certain Japanized European dishes, such as chicken nanban (fried chicken, pages 100–101) and nanban-zuke (escabeche, pages 104–105).

While living in Japan I saw myself as a modern version of these early mercantilists, striving to educate the Japanese while recognizing that, by their standards, I was strange and backward. So the word *nanban* captures this idea of a foreigner attempting to engage with Japanese culture, and it also perfectly describes the style of food I love to cook: very southern and a little bit barbaric.

"Japanese soul food" isn't my own phrase. I've shamelessly appropriated it from the Hakata ramen chain Ippudo, which once used it as a slogan. But it works for more than just ramen: besides coming from the south of Japan, as American soul food originates in the southern states, the recipes here are bold, hearty, unrefined and comforting. There are three fried chicken recipes in this book—if that ain't soul food, I don't know what is.

About this book

The recipes here are divided into seven sections: fundamentals, small dishes, large dishes, grilled items, ramen, desserts and drinks. I've avoided calling anything "starters" or "mains," because in an izakaya, the food comes all at once and is shared communally. Russell Norman puts it best in his Venetian cookbook *Polpo*: "Sharing is a social activity, very Mediterranean [or Asian] and makes a meal more like a feast—a convivial experience." True that, but obviously not every meal can be a dinner party, so most of the recipes here are written with full meals for two to four people in mind. As a general rule of thumb, two or three "small dishes" along with a heaped bowl of rice and perhaps a salad will be a meal for a couple or family with kids, whereas the "large dishes" can serve the same on their own.

Measurements are a mixture of weight and volume. In most cases, fudging the exact quantities will be absolutely fine, so if you taste something and you think it needs two teaspoons rather than one of mirin, then go ahead and add it.

Ingredients
What to Buy and Why to Buy It

Five Essential Items

Dashi powder
だしの素

Dashi, essentially a light broth made from dried seaweed and fish, is the fundamental flavor in Japanese cookery. Dishes that call for it will be noticeably lacking character and depth if it's omitted, and there's nothing that can really take its place. A stock made from smoked fish will do, but you're better off just getting a pack of dashi powder. It's available at any good Asian supermarket or from online suppliers, it's inexpensive and it's tremendously convenient. Also, it tastes great on french fries. If you buy a single Japanese ingredient, it should be this—or if you're really striving for authenticity and refinement, get the ingredients to make dashi from scratch—*kombu*, *katsuobushi* and dried shiitake (pages 38–39).

Miso (paste, not powder)
味噌

Miso is a paste made from fermented soybeans, rice, barley and/or other grains, and it has what I think of as a "complete" flavor: it's salty, umami-rich, sweet and a little sour, with lots of complex aromas running the gamut from fruity to earthy. There are countless varieties depending on the ingredients, types of mold, length of fermentation and texture, but they are generally (and roughly) divided into three main categories:

—— White (*shiro*) miso, made with a high proportion of white rice, tends to be light, sweet, salty and creamy tasting. The lighter color of white miso indicates that it's young and fresh—the flavor is more akin to a tangy chèvre than, say, a very old cave-aged Gruyère.

—— Red (*aka*) miso is darker in color than shiro miso, sometimes because of the ingredients used (such as brown rice or red beans), but more often because it has been aged longer. Over time, amino acids and sugars in the miso break down and react to become darker, more aromatic and distinctive compounds, giving it a richer, more complex flavor. Taken to an extreme, red miso can become a deep, chocolaty brown, as in the famous *Hatchō miso*. This delightfully rich miso has flavors of balsamic vinegar, Marmite, cocoa and toast.

—— "Mixed" (*awase*) miso is a catchall category that is somewhere between white and red, typically capturing the best of both worlds—the light, tangy, fruity freshness of white miso and the lingering, caramelly umami of red miso. This is the one I'd recommend you buy as I think it is the most versatile. I should note that you may come across miso soup powder in the supermarket. This stuff's not bad, but it isn't quite right as a substitute for actual miso paste, since it's the wrong consistency and it has other flavors in it. Also, when choosing a miso paste, try not to choose any that has dashi added—these are meant for stirring into hot water for a quick soup, but they'll add a fishy flavor to other dishes that call for plain miso. This would be especially unwelcome in something like miso caramel ice cream (page 210)!

Mirin
みりん

Mirin is a sweet cooking liquor, often described as "sweet sake," but it's actually closer to a sweetened, diluted *shochu*. It brings a mellow, tangy, honey-sweet flavor to dishes, not far off white port. If you've bought shochu, you can use that in its place (just add a little water and sugar), but mirin is easy to find and not very expensive, so you may as well get some. It's very versatile, and a must-have for most traditional Japanese recipes.

Shōyu (soy sauce)
醤油

Soy sauce comes in many, many forms, far beyond the "light" and "dark" varieties found at most supermarkets. But ignore the faux-Chinese stuff—most of the mainstream brands are just salty vinegar dyed brown and laced with MSG (check the ingredients if you don't believe me!). What you should get is a good-quality *shōyu*, the most basic and versatile type of Japanese soy sauce—Kikkoman is a good brand that's widely available, with a nice balance of richness, salt and tang. If you're gluten-free, get *tamari*—the flavor is a little richer because it's not brewed with wheat, but it's a good all-purpose substitute. Low-sodium shōyu tends to be surprisingly good as well.

Rice vinegar
米酢

Rice vinegar (*kome-zu*) brings a crisp, sweet acidity to brighten up all sorts of dishes, and, like dashi, it will bring a distinctly "Japanese" flavor to your cooking. You can substitute white wine or cider vinegar, but rice vinegar is widely available at large supermarkets these days. I prefer its smoother, cleaner flavor to any alternatives and generally use it as my go-to acidifier in any kind of cooking, not just Japanese. You may also want to try *genmai-su* (brown rice vinegar), which has a slightly richer flavor and is generally preferred by top-tier sushi chefs.

Southern Flavors

The five essential ingredients listed previously will give you a great foundation of Japanese flavors, but if you are keen to get a real taste of southern Japan, you might want to pick these up as well:

Yuzu-koshō
柚子胡椒

Yuzu-koshō is one of the most direct ways of giving your dishes a bold southern Japanese flavor. The name means "yuzu chili," and with just three ingredients—salt, fresh chilies and the zest of the *yuzu* citrus fruit—it packs a mighty punch. It's an unassuming green or red paste that's massively aromatic, with a spiky, permeating flavor that's like a blend of coriander, jalapeños, mandarin, lime and pine needles. Even though it's just chili and citrus, there's something irreplaceably unique about it (although the best comparison I've heard is that it's a bit like Indian lime pickle).

Shochu
焼酎

Shochu is the spirit of Kyushu and something you must try if you want to get an idea of what sets southern Japanese flavors apart. Rambunctiously boozy and flavorful, it's delicious on its own or in mixed drinks (see more in Drinks), but it also makes a fine substitute for sake if you dilute it with a little water, and it can replace *awamori* (rice whisky) in Okinawan recipes. Sweeter varieties can also replace mirin, although shochu is much more expensive, so you may not want to go crazy with it in your cooking.

More Key Ingredients
From Your Local Supermarket

Big supermarkets are pretty well stocked with foreign ingredients nowadays and usually have a modest but satisfactory section for Japanese food. Here are some bits you'll want to pick up on your next big shop.

Dried shiitake
干し椎茸

Drying shiitake concentrates their flavor and causes them to develop more of the umami compound called guanylate, which is why they make such satisfyingly rich stocks. Plus, they're a multitasker: once rehydrated, you can keep the resulting dashi and use the plumped-up mushrooms in your cooking. All recipes in this book that call for fresh shiitake, except for broiled mushrooms (pages 140–141), can also use rehydrated ones. Dried shiitake can be a little gritty; either rinse them in cold water before soaking, or pass the soaking liquid through strong paper towels or a coffee filter (see photo, page 40).

Toasted sesame oil
ごま油

Toasted sesame oil is a deep mahogany color and lends an intense nuttiness to dishes; whenever something seems to be lacking in richness, sesame oil is often the answer. Just be careful not to overuse it, and don't let it get too hot—it can burn easily and go acrid.

Toasted sesame seeds
いりごま

Sesame seeds are found at any supermarket but, annoyingly, almost always sold untoasted. This is very vexing, because the flavor of toasted sesame seeds is much different from that of the raw kind. The latter taste grassy and papery; the former, nutty and rich. However, they are easy to toast yourself: either spread them out in an even layer in a dry frying pan and gently heat them to a nice golden brown, or do the same in an oven set to 400°F. Keep your eye on them, because they can go from perfect to burnt in seconds.

Unrefined brown sugar
黒砂糖

In Japan, and Okinawa in particular, there is a prized type of unrefined cane sugar called *kokutō* or *kurozatō* ("black sugar") that is essentially a very dark muscovado sugar, and that's exactly what I use in its place. The flavor is quite similar—a wallop of date, prune, toffee and maple flavors. Better still is Billington's excellent molasses sugar, which has an intoxicatingly rich taste. South Asian jaggery is also a good substitute.

Rice
米

Japanese short-grain rice is usually sold as "sushi rice" at supermarkets. But it's not just for sushi; that's just how they sell it. A Japanese meal would be just plain weird if you use other kinds of rice like basmati or jasmine (minus 100 authenticity points), so pick some up and then read how to cook it properly (see pages 42–45).

Sake
日本酒

There are only a few recipes here that call for sake—most use mirin or shochu instead—but if you're looking to get a good grip on Japanese cooking fundamentals, you'll need this in your cupboard. Big supermarkets often sell just one brand—sometimes Sawanotsuru, sometimes Dragon. Both are fine for cooking. Not so much for drinking.

Udon
うどん

Udon are thick wheat noodles that are firmly kneaded to make them good and chewy. You can buy them fresh or dried at many supermarkets; I recommend the fresh ones, but either one is fine. You may need to soak fresh udon in cold water before using them, because they often come stuck together and have a tendency to break apart during cooking if they aren't separated beforehand.

Ramen
ラーメン

Ramen are basically Chinese-style egg noodles (see Alkaline Noodles, pages 158–159), which are available everywhere, but ideally, they should be fresh rather than dried. You may find fresh egg noodles in the supermarket, which are intended to be dumped into stir-fries. They'll do in a pinch, but they tend to overcook before you even open the bag. You're better off getting the dried kind and cooking them al dente, or better still, pick up some good-quality fresh noodles from a Chinese supermarket.

Tofu
豆腐

Tofu is often maligned for its starchy flavor and strange texture, but it's indispensable in certain recipes—sometimes merely as a bulking agent or texturizer and sometimes as a flavor sponge. For the recipes in this book, you should buy Japanese firm tofu—both "silken" or "block" are fine as long as they are firm—and you should gently extract their excess water before using. The easiest way to do this is to microwave them for about 10 seconds, but if, like me, you don't have a microwave, then simply place a small plate on top of your block of tofu for a half hour or so to gently squeeze out moisture.

More Key Ingredients
From Asian Stores

There are some ingredients that you just won't find at supermarkets, but the Internet is your best friend when it comes to special Japanese ingredients; there are several good Asian/Japanese online stores that deliver all over the country, often for a lower shipping charge than you might expect. For a full list of these suppliers, see pages 244–245.

Chili powder
一味唐辛子

You can use any old chili powder where recipes call for it, but I'd recommend getting a bag of hot Korean chili powder if you happen upon it. Actually more like tiny flakes than powder, it's richer, redder and, I think, altogether tastier than most supermarket varieties, which tend to be all blunt heat and not much flavor. Plus you'd get 20 bonus points for authenticity.

Yuzu juice
柚子果汁

You won't find many "luxury" ingredients in this book, but if you're going to splurge on one ingredient, it should be this. Yuzu is a hybrid citrus fruit renowned for its incomparable aroma, which is like a mix of lemon, mandarin, thyme, pine and grapefruit. I worked hard to come up with a decent substitute—a 2:1:1 mixture of lime, white grapefruit and orange juices was all right—but really, nothing can quite match the real McCoy. Which is a great source of exasperation, because this stuff is crazy expensive. I buy it wholesale for about $40 per liter (approximately 1 quart). If you find it at a Japanese grocer, it's likely to be more than twice that. The cheapest I've seen it at a shop, by a wide margin, was about $8.50 for 3⅓ ounces. Usually (yuzually?) it's closer to $14 for the same amount.

Such an expense sounds ridiculous, I'm sure. However, I would recommend that you buy a bottle at least once, just to understand the flavor. If you're unconvinced, there are ways to get that singular yuzu flavor into your food without the exorbitant cost. Yuzu-koshō (page 17) is a good option, though it also adds heat and salt. Yuzu liqueur also works (and it's lovely in a gin and tonic), but it is sweet. Occasionally I find yuzu salt, which is very tasty, and can contribute a good yuzu aroma for pennies per dish, but it lacks the same acidity as the juice, and besides, it's very rare. I don't recommend frozen or freeze-dried yuzu peel; something about the processing seems to dissipate its aroma, which means you have to use a lot of it, so ultimately it isn't cost-effective.

If a recipe calls for yuzu juice and you haven't any on hand, your best option is fresh lime juice, which has approximately the same acidity. Many recipes here use it for spark or balance first and aroma second, so don't feel like you can't make something if yuzu isn't an option.

Kombu
昆布

Japanese food without kombu is a little like French food without butter. It just doesn't make sense. Rich in umami compounds (especially natural MSG), kombu is a dried kelp that is most commonly infused in hot water to create dashi (pages 38–39), the fundamental Japanese stock. If you're really serious about Japanese cooking, you will need kombu in your cupboard, as well as katsuobushi (see below). But if you're just dabbling, or keen to cook Japanese food on an everyday basis, you're better off using dashi powder. I make dashi from scratch when I'm cooking for paying customers, but at home, it's dashi powder all the way.

Katsuobushi
鰹節

Katsuobushi means "katsuo shavings," *katsuo* being the Japanese word for a kind of small skipjack tuna, sometimes called bonito. It's a fascinating and delicious ingredient—wood-like shavings of petrified fish that has been smoked, fermented and dried multiple times. Its intense depth of flavor, used in conjunction with kombu, is what gives many Japanese dishes their delectable, soulful, smoky savoriness. However, it has some drawbacks for the home cook: it's expensive, it tends to lose its flavor quickly and it can be hard to track down, though most good Japanese or Asian supermarkets should have it. The fish itself is processed in Vietnam, but then gets shipped to the UK for shaving on a big, scary machine. This means it's fresher, cheaper and more widely available. They also sell clever katsuobushi products like the katsuo-pack, which is like a fish teabag, and katsuo powder—an inexpensive, sawdust-like by-product of shaving that gives a good, rich flavor for a fraction of the price.

Beni shōga
紅しょうが

Beni shōga means "red ginger," and that's what it is: julienned ginger that's been pickled in a mixture of vinegar, sugar, alcohol and various flavor enhancers and preservatives along with lots of red food dye. Traditionally, the red color comes from purple *shiso* and *umezu* (plum vinegar), but this method is now very rare. The artificial stuff is pretty good, though. If you've had *gari*, the thinly sliced pickled ginger served alongside sushi, that's pretty similar, but much sweeter. Beni shōga adds a pleasantly acidic zip to rich dishes like yaki-udon (pages 94–95) or yaki-curry. You can make it yourself by steeping julienned ginger in a mixture of rice vinegar, sugar, salt and beet juice.

Shichimi tōgarashi
七味唐辛子

This aromatic mostly chili spice blend is a favorite way to add piquancy to izakaya dishes. It's made from orange zest, sesame seeds, seaweed and other ingredients, so it isn't just pure heat. This is a lovely thing to have next to the stovetop or on the table to help dishes that need a little kick, and you can make it yourself if you like—the full recipe is on page 27.

Sanshō
山椒

Sanshō ("mountain pepper") are the young, green buds of Szechuan pepper, and provide a very similar flavor: lemony, gingery and distinctively tingly. Unlike Szechuan pepper, this is usually sold preground, and it's excellent sprinkled on fish or vegetable dishes.

Umeboshi
梅干し

Umeboshi are mercilessly sour, fermented, underripe apricots, often translated as "pickled plums." They've got an enormous amount of salt and acid, so much so that they used to angrily burn holes through Japanese lunch boxes, back when they were still made of tin. That's not to put you off, just to give you an idea of how intense they are; a little bit goes a long way. Often used to flavor plain rice (as in yaki-onigiri, pages 146–147), they're also great as an all-purpose acidifier, particularly good with vegetables. You can buy them whole or as a purée, and you can also find their lovely pink brine sold as a salty-sour vinegar called umezu. Look for the Clearspring brand in supermarkets and online; otherwise, head to your Asian grocer.

Kinako
きな粉

Kinako doesn't read well on paper: toasted soybean flour. Sounds like the domain of people with dietary issues. But it's actually really good; the flavor is like a mixture of malt and peanut butter, and it has a creamy consistency when mixed into liquids. It's pretty easy to get hold of, but it's also easy to make yourself, so long as you have a powerful food processor or blender. All you do is take dried soybeans and bake them until they're bronze and nutty-smelling, let them cool and process them to a powder in a food processor.

Vegetables and Fresh Herbs

Getting good Japanese vegetables is sometimes a challenge. However, there are some you should be able to find at any Japanese or Asian grocer, and some at large supermarkets or independent grocers.

Nira
にら

Nira is the Japanese word for kow choi, also called Chinese chives or garlic chives. The flavor is chive-like with a musk of garlic. Delicious. They turn up in a lot of recipes here, but if you can't get them, you can substitute chives plus a little minced garlic, or better yet, wild garlic. Sometimes you can find a lovely white version, or some with little flowers or flower buds—they taste the same, and are very pretty.

Daikon
大根

The big white radish called daikon ("big root"), more commonly known by its Hindi/Urdu name mooli, is an indispensable vegetable in Japanese cookery. Many large supermarkets now stock it. Because daikon are so large, you'll probably end up buying more than you need for any given recipe. Thinly slice the excess and chuck it in a jar with some vinegar, salt, sugar, ginger and chili for a delicious quick pickle.

Mushrooms: shiitake, eringi, enoki and shimeji
きのこ類：椎茸、エリンギ、えのき、しめじ

Shiitake are now commonplace in supermarkets, and so are shimeji—they're sold as beech mushrooms, and typically found in "exotic" selection packs. Eringi and enoki may require a trip to your local Chinatown, although the former can be replaced by oyster mushrooms and the latter are sometimes found in big supermarkets.

Shiso
しそ

Shiso is a wonderfully bold and aromatic herb, with a flavor sort of like a mix of clove, basil and mint, often used to garnish plates of sashimi. It's a little hard to come by, but it's now being grown in the UK and US so it turns up at farmers' markets and at specialty greengrocers from time to time. It does tend to be expensive, but if you live near a Vietnamese restaurant or supermarket, ask them if they can get it (it's called tía tô in Vietnamese). Their version is purple rather than green, but it's nearly as tasty and much cheaper.

1 —— udon	4 —— shichimi tōgarashi	7 —— white sesame	10 —— Japanese rice
2 —— brown sugar	5 —— Korean chili powder	8 —— umeboshi	11 —— kinako
3 —— yuzu juice	6 —— beni shōga	9 —— black sesame	12 —— shiso

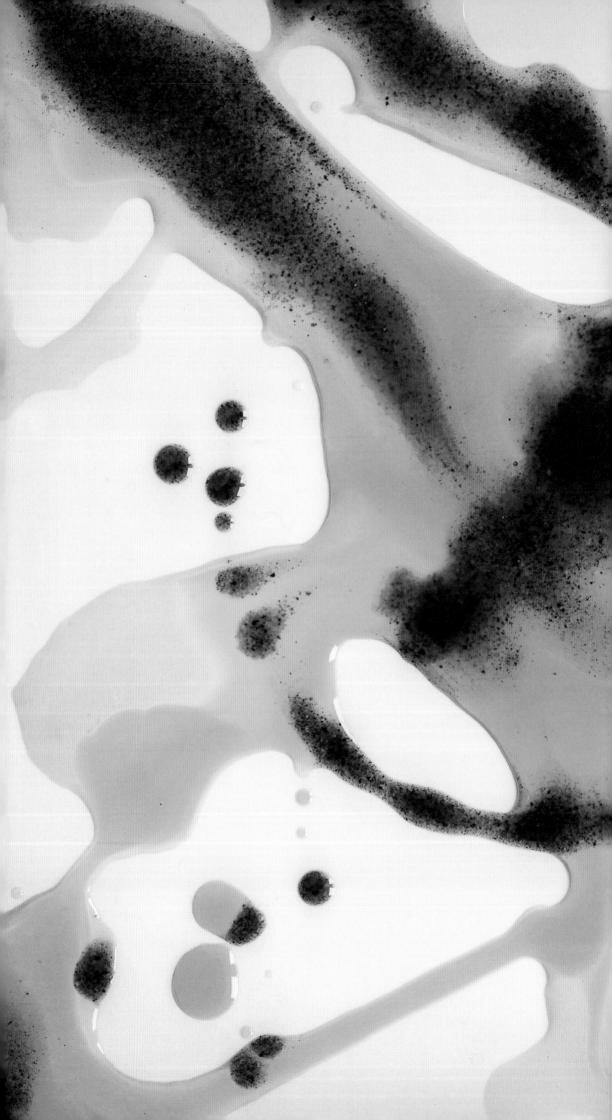

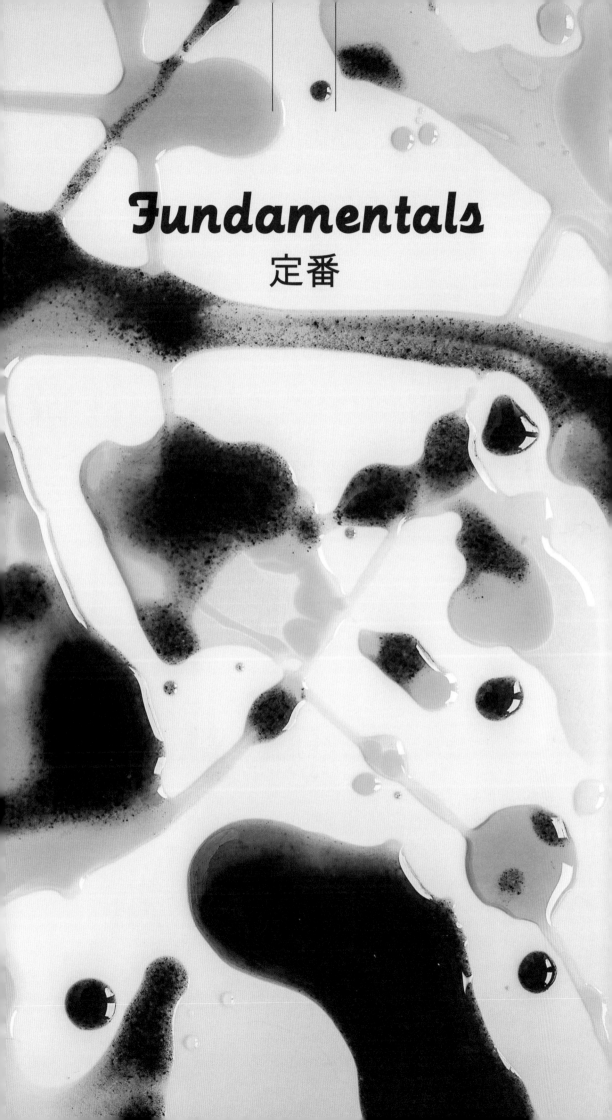

Fundamentals
定番

Basic Sauces
and Condiments

You'll find the following condiments and sauces referenced throughout this book, but you should get to know these even if you don't need them for a specific dish—they're good all-purpose Japanese soul food seasonings.

Sumiso

酢みそ

(Sweet-and-Sour Miso Dressing)

This sweet-and-sour miso dressing is very versatile. Diluted with a little oil and vinegar, it's a fantastic salad dressing, but on its own, it's also a wonderful flavoring for meat or fish. *Sumiso* tends to be quite salty because of all the miso, so if you're serving this, just be careful with your seasoning as you cook.

Yield:
about ⅞ cup (200ml)

Ingredients:
6 tbsp (100g) miso
2 tbsp rice vinegar
1 tbsp mirin
1–2 tsp sesame oil, to taste
superfine sugar, to taste
water, sake or dashi, to taste

Stir all the ingredients together and taste; add sugar if it's too sharp. The consistency should be pourable, but only barely—like Marmite, rather than peanut butter. If you need to thin it out, stir in little water, sake or dashi in small increments to taste.

Soy Sauce Tare

醤油ダレ

(All-purpose Sauce)

Tare (pronounced "tah-ray") is, broadly, a dipping sauce, and it comes in many flavors and varieties. Among the most popular are *negishio-dare* (salted scallion sauce), *goma-dare* (sesame sauce) and, perhaps the most versatile, *shōyu-dare*: soy sauce sauce. Alright, so it doesn't translate, but it is delicious: essentially sweetened and thickened soy sauce, flavored with a few aromatics. It's a great dip or glaze for all manner of broiled and grilled dishes (pages 120–147) and also makes a good teriyaki-ish marinade.

Yield:
about 1¼ cups (300ml)

Ingredients:
6½ tbsp (100ml) chicken stock
6½ tbsp (100ml) soy sauce
6½ tbsp (100ml) mirin

Ingredients *continued*:
2 tbsp (30g) brown sugar
1 clove garlic, crushed
¼–⅜ oz (5–10g) fresh ginger, sliced
big pinch white pepper
1 tsp cornstarch mixed with 1 tbsp cold water (optional)

Combine all the ingredients in a saucepan and bring to a simmer. Reduce by about a third. For a thicker sauce, whisk in the cornstarch slurry and cook for a few minutes to thicken. Pass through a sieve and keep in an airtight container in the fridge.

Ponzu
ポン酢

(Soy-Citrus Dipping Sauce)

Somewhat confusingly, "ponzu" can refer to citrus vinegar or the condiment made by combining it with soy sauce, as here. This is a simple but amazingly effective little soy-citrus dipping sauce—the acidity, salt and umami brighten up all sorts of savory dishes such as gyoza (pages 60–63), *satsuma-age* (pages 66–67) or tempura (pages 96–97).

Yield:
about ⅞ cup (200ml)

Ingredients:
⅝ cup (150ml) soy sauce
1 tbsp mirin
1 tbsp rice vinegar
juice of 2 limes or 1 lemon, or 2 tbsp yuzu
  juice
sugar, to taste—start with 1 tsp

Stir everything together in a jar or bowl until the sugar dissolves. Taste and add more sugar as needed. It should be quite sharp; the sugar is just to take the edge off, not to make the ponzu noticeably sweet.

Shichimi Tōgarashi
七味唐辛子

(Seven-flavor Chili Powder)

This aromatic blend is nearly as ubiquitous on Japanese restaurant tabletops as black pepper is over here. Any good Asian grocer will stock it, but if you'd rather make it yourself, here's how. Take these measurements as just a starting point—one benefit of making your own blend is that you can adjust the flavor however you like it. Keep it on hand to add a kick to rich, flavorsome recipes like rice yaki (pages 116–117) or yaki-curry (pages 90–91).

Yield:
makes 1 small jar

Ingredients:
2 tbsp sanshō (or finely ground
  Szechuan pepper)
2 tbsp dried orange peel (or yuzu
  or lemon peel)
4 tbsp chili powder—get the Korean stuff
  if you can
2 tbsp aonoriko (nori seaweed flakes)
2 tsp black sesame seeds
2 tsp hemp seeds
2 tsp garlic powder

Mix everything together and store in an airtight container.

Katsu Sauce
カツソース

(Sweet-and-Sour Brown Sauce)

Katsu sauce is often mistakenly thought of as curry sauce because of "katsu curry," a common dish of pork or chicken schnitzel served with Japanese curry. But "katsu" just refers to the schnitzel—it's short for *katsuretto*, the Japanized "cutlet"—and katsu sauce is actually more like a sweet-and-sour brown sauce with a distinct Worcestershire sauce-like flavor. Often referred to simply as *sōsu*, or "sauce," it's closely related to (and on most occasions, interchangeable with) *yakisoba* sauce and *okonomi* sauce. It's easy to find, but also easy to make. The choice is yours. Use as a topping for *tonkatsu* (pages 110–111), rice yaki (pages 116–117) or yaki-udon (pages 94–95), or as a general-purpose sauce for red meat. It's also amazing on french fries or with any dish that you'd usually serve with brown sauce.

Yield:
about ⅞ cup (200ml)

Ingredients:
6½ tbsp (100ml) ketchup
3 tbsp Worcestershire sauce
½ tbsp soy sauce
1 tbsp mirin
1 tbsp date syrup or dark brown sugar
1 tsp hot mustard (English or Japanese)
2 tsp tamarind purée (optional)
¼ tsp garlic powder
pinch white pepper

Mix everything together until smooth.

Māyu
マー油

(Flavored Oils)

Māyu is a common ramen topping in Kyushu made by charring garlic and then grinding it together with oil. I realize that burnt garlic made into an oil to pour over an already oily soup may not sound so good. But trust me, it is exquisite, and I often feel like tonkotsu ramen is missing something without it. Burning the garlic removes its sharpness and transforms it into something bittersweet and musky, matching the ramen's porky flavor perfectly. And the oil doesn't really make the soup feel any more greasy—just a little more slick and smooth. Plus, I love the way it dapples the surface of the broth in inky black droplets. The origins of the word māyu are unclear, though one theory suggests it's an abbreviation of the phrase mahō no yu, meaning "magic oil."

For Nanban I've developed a green oil as well, which wouldn't be called māyu in Japan, but it has no other name, so here it is. It's very different from the normal black māyu, with a refreshing, zesty quality. I've also included the recipe for red chili oil, which is called rāyu and simply means "spicy oil." This is set at the table as a condiment rather than used as a ramen topping.

Black Māyu
黒マー油

(Burnt Garlic Oil)

Yield:
about ⅞ cup (200ml)

Ingredients:
⅓ cup (75ml) vegetable oil
3¼ oz (90g) (about 1½ bulbs) garlic,
    peeled and roughly chopped
⅓ cup (75ml) sesame oil
1 tbsp (10g) black sesame seeds
pinch salt

Heat the vegetable oil and garlic in a saucepan and cook until the garlic is blackened—it should smell musky and smoky. Remove from the heat. Add the sesame oil to lower the temperature, then pureé along with the sesame seeds and salt in a blender or with a pestle and mortar until smooth and shiny. Pass through a fine sieve and leave to cool to room temperature. Store in a jar or bottle. Shake before using.

Green Māyu

青マー油

(Scallion Oil)

Yield:
about ⅝ cup (150ml)

Ingredients:
⅓ cup (75ml) vegetable oil
1 oz (25g) scallions, roughly chopped
¼–⅜ oz (5–10g) fresh ginger,
  peeled and finely chopped
1 clove garlic, peeled and finely
  chopped
⅓ cup (75ml) olive oil
pinch salt

Heat the vegetable oil in a saucepan until it feels warm when you hold your hand over it. Add the scallions, ginger and garlic and remove from the heat. Combine with the olive oil and salt in a blender and purée until smooth. Pass through a fine sieve and store in a jar or bottle. Shake before using.

Rāyu

ラー油

(Chili Oil)

Yield:
about 1¼ cups (300ml)

Ingredients:
⅞ cup (200ml) vegetable oil
6½ tbsp (100ml) sesame oil
¼–⅜ oz (5–10g) fresh ginger, peeled and
  sliced
4 cloves garlic
1 scallion
1 shallot, peeled
⅜ oz (10g) dried shrimp or anchovies
  (optional, but they add a lot of umami)
2 tbsp soy sauce
zest of ½ orange
1 oz (30g) dried red chilies or chili flakes

Heat the oils in a saucepan until it feels warm, but not hot, when you hold your hand over it. Chop the ginger, garlic, scallion, shallot and shrimp or anchovies (if using) into a fine mince—you can use a food processor or a mortar and pestle for this. Add this mixture to the warmed oil and cook until the shallots and garlic start to turn golden brown. Remove from the heat and allow to cool slightly, then add the soy sauce, orange zest and chilies. Transfer to an airtight jar, shake it up and leave to infuse for 24 hours. You can leave the bits to settle on the bottom and enjoy the clear oil on top, or you can simply stir them in and scoop them onto your food for extra texture and flavor. A must with gyoza (pages 60–63).

Kimchi
キムチ

Kimchi, of course, is Korean, not Japanese. But it turns up on a lot of Japanese menus, especially around Fukuoka, which is only a few hundred miles from Busan and has a large population of Korean immigrants. You can always buy kimchi, although making it is easy, and it's also more satisfying and much cheaper. Plus, you can adjust it to your taste—feel free to add more or less chili as well as other flavorings like dried seafood, citrus zest, fresh chilies or shiso. Here's how I make mine.

Once it's all packed down, the recipe here will fill a 2¼- to 2½-cup (500–600ml) jar, but it keeps for a very long time and is rather addictive. You'll get through it, and if not, give it away—people love pickles! Serve kimchi as a side to savory dishes like taco rice (pages 114–115), yaki-udon (pages 94–95) or *reimen* (pages 190–191). It also makes a great filling for *onigiri* (rice balls, pages 146–147).

Yield:
2¼–2½ cups (500–600ml)

Ingredients:
1 head Chinese cabbage
2 tbsp sea salt
2 tbsp chili powder (use Korean chili
    if you can)
1 tsp white pepper
1 scallion, sliced
¼–⅜ oz (5–10g) fresh ginger, finely julienned
2 cloves garlic, chopped

Cut the cabbage lengthwise into quarters, then again into ¾- to 1¼-inch (2–3cm) chunks. In a glass or plastic container, toss them together with everything else, squeezing, rubbing and bashing it all together to release their moisture. Let them sit for 30 minutes or so, then come back and bash and squeeze them some more; at this point, you should be able to wring them out like a wet sponge, creating a brine. Weight it all down with a heavy object that fits the container snugly—this could be a bottle of booze, another container filled with something heavy or a sealed plastic bag filled with water—whatever works. Make sure that enough juice has come out of the greens to submerge them, then cover loosely with a cloth or plastic wrap, securing with a string or rubber band to keep bugs out. Leave to sit at room temperature for 5–6 days (less if it's warm in your kitchen, more if it's cold).

Have a look and a taste. When it's noticeably sour, it's ready—remove the weight and transfer to the fridge, where it will keep for weeks.

Braised Kombu
昆布の佃煮

If you're making dashi from scratch (pages 38–39)—plus 20 authenticity points and a gold star for you—you may end up with a fair amount of leftover kombu. You needn't throw this away; it can be chopped up and added to stews or soups, or it can be prepared as a sort of braised jam called *tsukudani*, a popular method for preserving all sorts of seafood. Cooked way down in soy sauce and sugar, the end product reminds me a bit of braised red cabbage. It's very salty, sweet and delicious, making it a perfect accompaniment to rice or a filling for onigiri (pages 146–147).

Yield:
6 tbsp (100g)

Ingredients:
1 big piece rehydrated kombu
    (from making dashi)
2 tbsp soy sauce
1 tbsp sugar
1 tbsp mirin
1 tsp rice vinegar
1²⁄₃ cups (400ml) water
1 tsp sesame seeds

Cut the kombu into strips about 1½ inches (4cm) wide, then julienne them, like you would if preparing cabbage for slaw. Add to a saucepan with the soy sauce, sugar, mirin, vinegar and water, and bring to the boil. Reduce the heat to medium—it should be between a simmer and a full boil—and cook until the liquid reduces to a thick, sticky glaze.

Taste the kombu; it should be quite soft but not mushy. If it needs more cooking, add a little water and carry on. Make sure there is no liquid left; it should be a glaze rather than a sauce or syrup. When the kombu is ready, stir in the sesame seeds. Leave to cool before using as a filling for onigiri or as a topping for rice.

Ume-shiso Cucumber
梅しそキュウリ

The combination of devilishly sour umeboshi (pickled plums) and peppery, minty shiso is one of Japan's favorite flavorings, used in everything from popcorn to spaghetti. It's incredibly potent, something that flies in the face of the common misconception that Japanese food is always delicate and restrained. This makes a perfect filling for onigiri (pages 146–147)—a little goes a long way in seasoning rice. And it also tastes great in a toasted cheese sandwich.

Yield:
about 3¼ oz (90g), enough to fill 4 onigiri

Ingredients:
¼ cucumber, seeds removed, cut into
    small dice
4 umeboshi, roughly chopped, or 4–5 tsp
    umeboshi purée
6 leaves shiso, chopped
1 tbsp spent katsuobushi (from making dashi),
    squeezed dry and roughly chopped
    (optional)

Stir everything together and use to fill onigiri following the instructions on page 147.

Dashi
出汁

If you are keen to explore traditional Japanese cookery, how to make dashi is perhaps the very first thing you should learn. Its smoky, briny, slightly sweet taste is the fundamental flavor of innumerable Japanese dishes, a deep yet subtle backdrop that brings other ingredients into stark relief.

Dashi is classically made with one essential ingredient at its core: kombu. Kombu is dried kelp, simple as that. The drying process concentrates its flavor, which it then relinquishes generously when bathed in hot water. It is extraordinarily rich in glutamic acid, which registers on our palate as the subtle but quintessential basic taste known as umami. The term was coined in the early 1900s by a chemist named Kikunae Ikeda—he was trying to determine what compound was responsible for the "umami" of his wife's dashi—literally, "delicious taste."

In the years to come, two other umami-producing compounds would be discovered that work synergistically with glutamic acid: guanylate and inosinate. The former is most readily extracted from dried shiitake mushrooms, and the latter from dried meat or fish, especially katsuobushi. Katsuobushi is a remarkable product and the second essential ingredient in most dashi. It is made through a complicated process in which the loins of small tuna called katsuo are repeatedly smoked, fermented and dried until they resemble chunks of dark driftwood. This is then shaved thinly into katsuobushi, which has an irresistible smoked fish aroma and an enormously complex flavor from the fermentation.

Typically, dashi made with kombu and katsuobushi doesn't include shiitake. However, I use it for two reasons: I think the extra umami and rich, meaty flavor it provides make the dashi taste better, and it allows me to use a little less katsuobushi, which is really expensive. It's a win-win!

Having said all of this, you can always use the powdered stuff. Seriously. I do it, mainly because Kyushu-style dashi is actually made with flying fish rather than katsuo, and in the UK I have only been able to source powdered flying fish dashi and not actual dried flying fish. In truth, powdered dashi is a mainstay of any Japanese home kitchen, and it's really far tastier than our Western analogue, the dreaded bouillon cube. So make fresh dashi if you have the time and ingredients (it is better and important to learn) but nobody will judge you if you use powdered dashi instead. I promise. Shizuo Tsuji writes, in his essential *Japanese Cooking: A Simple Art*: "While some instant mixes are excellent, and none is bad, nothing compares in subtle flavor and delicate fragrance with dashi made from freshly shaved bonito."

I should note the same cannot be said for replacing proper ramen broth with anything endorsed by Marco Pierre White!

Yield:	Ingredients:
about 2¼ cups (500ml)	⅜ oz (10g) kombu
	¾ oz (20g) dried shiitake
	2½ cups (600ml) Volvic mineral water
	⅜ oz (10g) katsuobushi

This will sound silly, but it's true: if you want to make great dashi, use bottled water. Volvic, to be precise. The fact is that most tap water here in the UK is way too hard; for reasons I don't quite understand, the excess minerals in our water interfere with the extraction and infusion of compounds in the kombu, shiitake and katsuobushi. And sure enough, I was unhappy with my dashi made with London's finest. One day I tried it with Volvic—the lowest-mineral bottled water I could find—and the results were like night and day. Baristas and brewers have similar things to say about water in coffee or beer. However, this is all very silly, isn't it, using Volvic to make broth? When I'm cooking for just me, I don't bother. My dashi comes out good enough for most things when I use tap water. But if I've got a guest to impress, or if I'm making something where the dashi is front and center—say sōki soba (pages 184–185)—then I reach for the Volvic for sure.

Rinse the kombu and shiitake under running water, place in a saucepan and pour the mineral water over them. Very gently bring the water to a simmer, then remove from the heat. Add the katsuobushi and leave to infuse for at least 30 minutes—let it cool to room temperature. Pass through a fine sieve over a pitcher or bowl, keeping the spent ingredients to make *niban dashi*—a somewhat fishier but lighter stock made by simmering the pre-used kombu, mushrooms and fish flakes in water for about 30 minutes, then reducing until the desired strength of flavor is achieved. Considering how expensive katsuobushi is, this is a very cost-effective way to get a large quantity of dashi.

Vegetarian Dashi
ベジタリアン出汁

If you're a vegetarian or you just can't get katsuobushi, this dashi is an excellent alternative. Keep the spent kombu to make braised kombu (pages 34–35) and pickle the spent shiitake in rice vinegar, mirin and soy sauce, or use it in a recipe.

Yield:
about 2¼ cups (500ml)

Ingredients:
⅜ oz (10g) kombu
¾ oz (20g) dried shiitake
2½ cups (600ml) water

Rinse the kombu and shiitake under running water, place in a saucepan and pour the water over them. Very gently bring the water to a simmer, then remove from the heat. Leave to infuse for at least 30 minutes—let it cool to room temperature. Pass through a fine sieve set over a jug or bowl—alternatively use a coffee filter. You can also make this dashi by simply combining all the cold ingredients together and leaving them to infuse overnight.

Left: Using a coffee filter is an excellent way to clarify your dashi.

How to Cook Japanese Rice

Most of the recipes in this book—and in Japanese gastronomy generally—are meant to be eaten with a panful of rice to complete the meal. I read somewhere that traditional Japanese food has no center—there are no main courses and no main ingredients—but it has a "destination," and that destination is rice. So you'd better learn to cook it or you'll never get there. Cooking rice is something that couldn't be simpler—and couldn't be easier to screw up. Supposedly fail-safe recipes can go terribly wrong even when followed to the letter—this is because everybody's pans, lids, stovetops, tap water, rice and measuring cups are a little different.

So what I'm going to do is present the method and measurements that work for me—and they work every time. But if they don't work for you, and they might not, I'm also including some troubleshooting tips to help you nail it. Cooking perfect rice takes practice, and you have to eliminate variables if you want to improve. So I would recommend always using the same brand of rice and always using the same pan; that way, it's really a matter of simply adjusting the water content and heat. If you are already happy with how your Japanese rice is turning out, then don't even bother reading this—I don't want to interfere with your tried-and-true method. You should hold on to that forever.

I should note that this method works only *up to a certain quantity*—about 3⅓ pounds (1.5kg) of rice—before it starts to become uneven, with some rice overdone and some rice under. You can minimize uneven cooking by choosing a pan that may seem a little too big for the amount of rice you're preparing; bear in mind that rice farther away from the heat source at the bottom of the pan will take more time to cook, so you want to minimize the height of the rice in your pan. However, this generally applies only if you're cooking really large quantities; for ordinary family-size servings, you are not likely to have any issues with unevenness.

Note that if you have a rice cooker, simply follow the instructions and measurements that come with it.

Ratios for cooking rice are as follows:

By weight: 1 part rice to 1.3 parts water
(e.g., 5⅓ oz [150g] rice to 6⅞ oz [195g] water)
By volume: 1 part rice to 1.1 parts water
(e.g., ¾ cup [180ml] to ⅞ cup [198ml] water)

(Note: These measurements aren't arbitrary; ¾ cup [180ml] is a Japanese cup, and 5⅓ oz [150g] is the approximate weight of 1 Japanese cup of rice.)

I almost always measure by weight. It's more accurate and easier if you're cooking large quantities. You will need roughly 2 oz (60g) uncooked rice per serving, or 2½ oz (75g) if you're quite hungry (or if you really like rice, like I do). If you're making yaki-onigiri (pages 146–147), you'll need about 1–1½ oz (30–40g) per ball.

Measure out your rice into a deep saucepan with a snug-fitting lid. Wash it by filling up the saucepan with cold water, then rubbing and swishing the rice around to rinse off excess starch. Drain off the cloudy water; you may want to use a sieve for this, but you can also just carefully tilt the pot so the water runs out but the rice stays put. Repeat this process 3 or 4 times. Most cookbooks say you should do this "until the water runs clear," but in reality you would have to use 9 or 10 changes of water if you're expecting it to look like something out of a bottled water advert. Realistically, the water should just be pretty clear; that is, it should look more like cloudy water than watery milk. Here's what Roy Choi, LA chef extraordinaire and inventor of the Korean taco, has to say about washing rice:

The most important step in cooking rice is how you wash it . . . Wash your rice to cleanse, not to clean. Run cold water through the rice and massage the grains, transferring all your energy to the rice as the rice transfers its own energy to you. Try to feel every single grain as you swirl the water.

Pretty spiritual stuff. But actually (I'm going to lose points for saying this), not washing your rice at all won't have that much of a discernible impact on the finished product. It will be a little bit pastier; the grains will be covered in a thin, starchy film. But unless the Japanese ambassador is coming to dinner, and you're in a hurry (or just feeling lazy), don't worry about washing the rice. It will be fine. (I can sense my Japanese mother-in-law clairvoyantly shaking her head as I write this.) I always wash rice for paying customers; for myself, only if I'm in the mood.

Cover the washed rice with the appropriate amount of water (see ratios above) and swirl the pan to make sure the rice is distributed in an even layer. Place a lid on the pan, and set over a medium-high heat on a burner that's not too wide and not too narrow—it should fit the pan you're using. Bring the water to the boil, then immediately reduce the heat to as low as possible. Set a timer for 18 minutes, then go do something else. Don't stir or take the lid off the rice; you need to keep the moisture in until it's all absorbed. When the timer goes off, go check on the rice and fluff it with a fork or rice paddle; dig deep to vertically redistribute the grains and to check the consistency of the rice on the bottom. Put the lid back on the pan and let the rice sit, off the heat, for another 5 minutes; this will let the heat redistribute, and any residual moisture will be absorbed into the rice. This should give you perfect rice. But if not . . .

Rice Troubleshooting: Common Problems

My rice is too hard.

The water is evaporating too quickly as it steams, so try a smaller burner and a slightly longer cooking time (about 20 minutes cooking, plus 5 minutes resting with the lid on). Alternatively, add a little more water at the beginning of cooking; try a ratio of 1 to 1.4 by weight, so $5\frac{1}{3}$ oz (150g) rice with $7\frac{1}{2}$ oz (210g) water. If this doesn't help, check to see that your lid isn't letting too much steam out; if it is, find one that fits more snugly, or else you can wrap the lid in a clean tea towel before setting it on the pan, which creates a better seal.

My rice is mushy or gluey.

Use less water. If your rice is only a touch too gluey or sticky but otherwise has a good texture, this can often be remedied by washing the rice beforehand.

My rice is too hard but there's also still a lot of starchy water in the pan.

This usually means that your ratios and temperature are right, but you need to cook the rice longer; try 20–25 minutes.

My rice is mushy (or burnt) on the bottom but underdone on top.

This is usually caused by either a flame that is too hot, or a pan that is too small. If your rice is burning on the bottom before it's cooked through, you need to set it on a smaller burner/lower heat; if it's cooking unevenly, try a wider pan so the rice isn't piled up too high. Note: If your rice is cooked well but it has developed a golden-brown crust on the bottom, consider this a bonus! The crunchy bits are delicious and are actually desirable in certain Japanese rice dishes.

Small Dishes
一品料理

Baked Sweet Potato
with Yuzu Butter
焼き芋柚子バター和え

A really old-school, really simple snack sold on Japanese backstreets and at festivals is the humble *yaki-imo*: baked sweet potato. Traditionally these are cooked in their skins on hot stones, retaining all their moisture and sweetness. They are typically served unadorned and eaten with your hands. I remember walking home from the railway station on many a drunken evening, drawn into a detour to the yaki-imo truck by the vendor's call and the irresistible aroma of his wares. It was like the visible steam in old cartoons that lifts characters off their feet and floats them toward the source.

I serve these with a little butter mixed with yuzu and soy sauce—all the sweet potatoes need to turn them into an indulgent, hearty side. This will likely make more yuzu butter than you need. You can scale down the recipe if you like, but I think you'll fall in love with this stuff and surely think of other things to do with it (it is amazing, for example, on corn).

Yield:

6 servings

Ingredients:

14 tbsp (200g) butter, at room temperature
1 ½ tbsp yuzu juice
1 tbsp soy sauce
6 sweet potatoes
black sesame seeds, crushed, to garnish

Beat together the butter, yuzu juice and soy sauce until completely homogenized and no droplets of liquid remain (you may want to use an electric mixer for this, but start off beating gently or the liquid will spatter everywhere). Pack into a container and chill until set.

Heat the oven to 350°F. Scrub the sweet potatoes and cut off any eyes or gnarly bits. Bake them for 45–60 minutes, depending on their size—they're done when you can easily poke all the way through their thickest part with a chopstick. Leave the potatoes to cool slightly.

Cut the yuzu butter into chunks (about 1 tbsp [15g] per potato). Split open the sweet potatoes and put a generous knob of the yuzu butter inside each. Garnish with a sprinkle of sesame seeds and serve immediately.

Karashi Mentaiko

辛子明太子

(Chili-cured Pollock Roe)

A handful of local specialties in Japan have become so popular that they have graduated to national icons, migrating from the souvenir stands in their hometown railway stations to Narita airport, ready to be flown away to Japanese expats hungry for a taste of home. One of these über-specialties is karashi mentaiko, from the Fukuoka district of Hakata. Originating from a Korean tradition of salted, spiced, fermented seafood, this is the roe of the *mentai*, a fish similar to pollock, that has been cured in a mixture of chili, salt and other seasonings. It's fishy, salty, spicy, umami-rich and a little sweet, and it's absolutely delicious in spite of its somewhat grotesque, veiny appearance.

Enjoy mentaiko raw or grilled on top of plain rice, in onigiri (pages 146–147), stuffed into sardines (pages 142–143) or mixed into pasta (pages 86–87). Some Kyushu ramen shops even offer it as an optional topping to give the broth a fishy-spicy kick. It also makes a mean *taramasalata*!

Pollock and haddock roe can be pretty tough to find, to be honest. It's in season from around January to March, and even then you'll likely have to ring up your fishmonger ahead of time. However, you can often find mentaiko at Japanese or Korean supermarkets, typically frozen. It's a little pricy, but most of the time it will be your only option for real mentaiko. That said, it's easy and inexpensive to make yourself, so try it if you can. This recipe calls for *gochujang*, which is a delicious Korean fermented rice and chili paste—like miso, but spicy.

Yield:
about 10½ oz (300g)

Ingredients:
1 tbsp salt
1 tsp dashi powder (optional)
1 tbsp soy sauce
1 tbsp mirin

Ingredients *continued*:
1 tbsp shochu (or sake)
1 tbsp rice vinegar
1 oz (30g) gochujang (fermented Korean chili-rice paste) or ⅓ oz (10g) hot chili powder (or more or less, to taste)
10½ oz (300g) fresh pollock or haddock roe

Combine the salt, dashi powder (if using), soy sauce, mirin, shochu (or sake), vinegar and gochujang (or chili powder). Rub this mixture all over the roes, ensuring that they are evenly covered. Refrigerate for 24–48 hours to cure. Once cured, this will keep for about 3 days in the fridge, or for several months in the freezer.

Faux Mentaiko

Because prepared mentaiko is rare and expensive in the UK, and pollock/haddock roe is only available for a few months out of the year, I've had to experiment with alternatives. This is the best version I've come up with, using a Swedish cod roe spread that comes in a funny toothpaste-tube-type container. This is widely available online or at continental delis, and even from Ocado. The taste is appropriately fishy and salty; it's also faintly smoky, which renders the flavor inauthentic, but still quite delicious.

Yield:
about 7 oz (200g)

Ingredients:
1 6¾-oz (190g) tube Kalles Kaviar or similar smoked cod roe spread
1 tbsp Korean chili powder or about ½ oz (15g) gochujang

Mix the roe and the chili together until well combined. Cover, keep refrigerated and consume within a few days.

Mackerel Kake-ae

鯖のかけ和え

(Vinegar-cured Mackerel with Vegetables and Sweet Miso)

This light and healthy recipe comes from Saga prefecture, to the southwest of Fukuoka. It is one of the smallest prefectures in Japan and very rural, and frequently made fun of for being boring and backward, even by Saga natives. So although I dated a girl who lived there for three months, I didn't spend a great deal of time in Saga, and I didn't get to know the food very well. Plus, she broke my heart, so I tend to associate Saga and its food with bad memories. But at some point, I realized that I had no Saga dishes on my menu, and that seemed unfair. This simple cured fish salad filled not only a geographic gap but also a culinary one; I didn't have many dishes in my repertoire that could be described as "light." I often describe this dish as ceviche, Kyushu-style.

Yield:
4–6 servings

Ingredients:
For the fish:
14–17½ oz (400–500g) mackerel fillets (about 1 fillet per serving)
⅞ cup (200ml) rice vinegar
½ tsp salt
2¼ tsp (10g) sugar
2 tsp mirin
½ tsp soy sauce

For the sweet miso sauce:
1½ tbsp (15g) toasted sesame seeds
2½ tbsp (40ml) curing liquid (see method)
3¼ tbsp (50ml) mirin
1 tsp sesame oil
3¼ tbsp (65g) white or awase miso

For the vegetables:
½ daikon (mooli), peeled
3½ oz (100g) carrot, peeled
salt
2 oz (60g) cucumber

To serve:
⅓ oz (10g) chives, finely chopped
sesame seeds, to garnish

For the fish:
Remove pin bones and the tough outer skin from the mackerel; these are fiddly but necessary jobs. To remove the skin, place the fillet, skin side down, on your cutting board, and cut through the flesh near the tail end, but don't slice through the skin. Then you can grab the skin and peel it away in one sheet. It takes some practice, but don't worry if you mangle the first few fillets—you can still use them. Cut the prepared mackerel into bite-size chunks, about ⅜ inch (1cm) thick, and put in a bowl. Mix all the remaining ingredients together, ensuring that the salt and sugar have dissolved, and pour over the mackerel pieces. Refrigerate for 4 hours, tossing the fish halfway through to redistribute. Drain and reserve the curing liquid.

For the sweet miso sauce:
Crush the sesame seeds to a rough powder using a mortar and pestle, then mix well with the remaining ingredients in a bowl. The dressing needn't be completely smooth, just well mixed.

For the vegetables:
Cut the daikon and carrot into thin strips, about ⅓ inch (8mm) wide and no more than ¹⁄₁₆ inch (2mm) thick. Salt them liberally and leave to drain for 1 hour—this extracts water from the vegetables to improve their texture while also seasoning them, and removes bitterness from the daikon. Rinse in 2 or 3 changes of cold water, then taste them—if they're too salty, keep rinsing. Cut the cucumber in half lengthwise and remove the seeds, then slice into half-moon shapes as thinly as possible (use a mandoline if you have one).

To serve:
Toss the fish with the vegetables and the sweet miso sauce. Pile into small bowls and garnish with chives and a few sesame seeds.

Onsen Tamago

温泉玉子

(Hot Spring Eggs)

温泉玉子

Onsen tamago means "hot spring eggs." And that's exactly what they are: eggs cooked in a hot spring. All around Japan's hot spring resorts you'll find these eggs, which take advantage of the peculiar fact that egg yolks set and solidify at a lower temperature than egg whites—so the end product has a softly jellified white and a creamy, semisolid yolk.

But you don't need a hot spring to achieve this remarkable effect. All you need is either a temperature-controlled water bath or an immersion circulator, or an oven and a reliable thermometer. They're excellent on their own with a little ponzu (pages 26–27) or just soy sauce, and they make a great topping for all sorts of savory dishes such as yaki-curry (pages 90–91) and hunter ramen (pages 188–189).

Yield:
4–6 eggs

Ingredients:
4–6 eggs
plenty of water

For an immersion circulator or water bath:

Heat your water to 145°F. Lower the eggs into the water (a sieve or noodle basket helps with this) and leave them there for 1 hour. Take them out, and that's it; crack them open and the cooked eggs will slip right out of their shells. Serve while still warm, in dashi, or as a topping for other dishes.

For an oven:

Preheat your oven to 150°F. Boil some water and pour it into an ovenproof dish and leave it to cool to 150°F. Lower in the eggs and place in the oven. Leave them in there for about an hour, checking the temperature of the water with a thermometer periodically to make sure it doesn't exceed 150°F and doesn't drop below 140°F. After an hour, test one egg; they're good to go when the white is like a soft jelly.

Buta Kakuni Manjū

豚角煮まんじゅう

(Pork Belly Buns)

Buta kakuni manjū are Japan's take on *gua bao*, the Taiwanese pork buns recently popularized by Momofuku and sometimes called "Hirata buns." This nomenclature isn't found in Japan; it actually comes from Masashi Hirata, the executive chef of Ippudo in New York. Pretty cheeky, if you ask me, slapping your name on a dish that has been around for eons. Maybe I'll start calling cheeseburgers "Anderson buns." Anyway, these aren't exactly Japanese, but they are a common street snack in Nagasaki's Chinatown, where they're served directly out of big bamboo steamers, billowing their enticing aroma into the lantern-lit alleyways. I wanted to bring the Chinese roots of this dish to the fore, so I've used some aromatics in the simmering liquid that impart a captivating complexity to the pork. They will also perfume your house and make it smell like your favorite Cantonese restaurant.

Yield:

4 servings

Ingredients:
For the pork belly:
2 tbsp vegetable oil
17½ oz (500g) pork belly, rind removed
(save it for tonpi, pages 58–59)
water, as required
1 onion, cut into quarters
2 cloves garlic
⅓ oz (10g) ginger, sliced
2 star anise
2 bay leaves
1 stick (1½–2 inches [4–5cm]) cinnamon
1¼ cups (300ml) dashi

Ingredients *continued*:
2 tbsp (30ml) mirin
1 tbsp superfine sugar
2 tbsp (30ml) soy sauce—use a really
rich-flavored one, like tamari,
koikuchi or even *ketjap manis*

To serve:
8–10 plain buns, sliced, for steaming
(check your Chinese grocer's freezer
section—they will be labeled
mantou or "doubled slice")
½ leek, julienned
¼ cup (60ml) hoisin sauce
½ cucumber, thinly sliced
hot mustard, to taste (optional)

For the pork belly:
Heat the vegetable oil in a deep casserole dish. Brown the pork belly over a medium-high heat on all sides. Remove the meat and drain the fat from the pan. Return the pan to the heat and put the pork back in. Cover with water and add the onion, garlic, ginger, star anise, bay leaves and cinnamon. You need to keep the pork submerged in the cooking liquid; I put a metal bowl weighted down with a bottle of water on top of the meat in the pan. Bring the liquid to the boil, and then reduce the heat to a bare simmer; it should only just be bubbling. Simmer for 2 hours, topping up with water if necessary. The pork should be quite soft, but not falling apart.

Remove the pork and drain off the cooking liquid (hold on to it if you want to—it's a pretty good stock base). Clean the pan, and pour in the dashi, mirin and sugar. Bring the liquid to the boil. Slice the pork belly into chunks, about ⅜–⅝ inch (10–15mm) thick. Add these to the dashi and reduce the heat to medium-low—it should simmer a little more than the initial

braise, but only just. Let the liquid reduce, basting the meat often, until it's syrupy, then add the soy sauce and reduce a little more. Be patient here—it will take a good 30–40 minutes to reduce. Don't be tempted to turn the heat up, as this will make the meat go dry. The pork is done when it's coated in a sticky, dark brown glaze. This is even better if you leave the pork in its glaze in the fridge overnight; it's like a sort of post-marinade. But it takes a fair bit of willpower not to indulge immediately!

To serve:
Steam the buns in a steamer basket lined with parchment paper, or in a very hot oven with a tray of boiling water placed at the bottom. Gently reheat the buta kakuni in its own glaze. Stuff the pork into the buns along with the leek, hoisin sauce, cucumber and a thin spread of mustard, if you like. You can keep these nice and hot in the steamer until ready to serve.

Tonpi
豚皮

(Okinawa-style Pork Cracklings)

Pork cracklings aren't common in Japan, though they are enjoyed in Okinawa, famous for its nose-to-tail pig cuisine. But if you've made *chāshū* (pages 162–163) or buta kakuni (pages 56–57), then you'll have some skin left over, and it would be a shame to waste it.

Yield:		Ingredients:
2–4 servings		½–¾ lb (200–300g) pork skin
		sea salt
		oil, for frying
		MSG (or more sea salt)
		black pepper
		shichimi powder
		¼ lemon, cut into wedges

Heat the oven to 225°F. Boil the pork skin for about 30 minutes to tenderize it and to render off some of the fat. Leave to dry on a wire rack, then cut into strips about ¾ inch (2cm) wide. Rub with sea salt and spread out on a baking sheet rubbed with oil, and place in the oven to dehydrate for 3–4 hours. Check the skins every hour or so; if they're getting greasy, drain the fat and blot them dry; if they're getting too brown in spots, turn them over.

Remove the skins from the oven, blot off any excess fat and leave to cool and air-dry on a wire rack. They should be really hard, like lacquer; they should resist bending and make a nice thunk when you whack them against the counter. Heat some oil to 325°F. Fry the skins until puffy and golden brown, then drain on paper towels and season generously with MSG, pepper and shichimi. Serve with a wedge of lemon.

Gyoza

餃子

Gyoza are an izakaya icon. They're also the most common and popular side dish with ramen, like fries with a burger. Everyone does them a little differently, but they should always be full of texture, umami and spice, and as London burger authority Daniel Young once said of french fries, they should be "too hot to eat right away, but too good not to."

Pork Gyoza

豚肉餃子

Yield:

24 gyoza

Ingredients:

10½ oz (300g) ground pork (avoid lean meat; it's too dry)

½ oz (15g) fresh ginger, finely chopped

1 scallion, finely chopped

Ingredients *continued*:

1 clove garlic, finely chopped

½ tsp white pepper

½ tsp salt or MSG

24 gyoza wrappers

oil, for frying

splash of water (or sake), for steaming

Combine everything but the gyoza wrappers in a bowl—use your hands, it's the only way. Make sure all the seasonings are evenly distributed throughout, but don't overwork it so it becomes pasty. Fill a little dish with water. Use a spoon to portion out the mixture onto each gyoza wrapper, then wet your fingertips in the water and run them along the edges of each wrapper. Draw up the sides and press them firmly together to enclose the filling, and crimp them 3 or 4 times. Heat a glug of oil in a frying pan to a medium heat and add the gyoza—you may have to do them in batches to make sure they're all flat against the surface of the pan. Cook for about 3 minutes on each side, until golden brown. At the end of cooking, add a splash of water or sake to the pan and cover with a lid immediately so the gyoza steam through; ideally, the wrappers should take on two different textures from this method: crisp from the frying and supple from the steaming. Serve with ponzu (pages 26–27) and some rāyu (page 31).

Shrimp Gyoza

エビ餃子

Yield:

24 gyoza

Ingredients:

12 oz (350g) raw shrimp, shelled, deveined and roughly chopped

2 scallions (or nira), thinly sliced

⅓ oz (10g) fresh ginger, finely chopped

Ingredients *continued*:

1 clove garlic, finely chopped

2 pinches white pepper

½ tsp salt or MSG

juice of ¼ lime

24 gyoza wrappers

oil, for frying

splash of water (or sake), for steaming

I like the shrimp in my gyoza to have a lot of texture, so I chop them by hand and leave them nice and chunky. It also saves having to wash the food processor.

Chop the shrimp with a cleaver or other sharp, heavy knife, then mix together with everything else except the wrappers. Fill, seal and cook the gyoza as above.

Vegetable Gyoza

野菜餃子

Yield:
12 gyoza

Ingredients:
2 tbsp sesame oil
3½ oz (100g) mushrooms (ideally shiitake,
    but any will do), diced
¼ Chinese cabbage, shredded
½ leek, cut into quarters lengthwise and
    then thinly sliced
⅓–½ oz (10–15g) fresh ginger, finely
    chopped
1 clove garlic, finely chopped
2 pinches white pepper
2 tsp yuzu-koshō (optional—substitute
    a little lime juice and chili powder if you like)
salt, to taste (optional)
2 scallions (or nira), thinly sliced
1 tbsp miso or sumiso (pages 24–25)
12 gyoza wrappers
oil, for frying
water (or sake), for steaming

Heat the sesame oil in a frying pan, then add the mush-rooms, Chinese cabbage, leek, ginger and garlic. Cook over a moderate heat for about 10 minutes or until everything is tender, but not mushy. Add the pepper, yuzu-koshō and salt (if using), then stir in the scallions and miso and cook for another 2–3 minutes; if the mixture looks too dry, add a splash of water, but let it evaporate completely as the vegetables finish cooking. Leave the vegetable mixture to cool, then fill, seal and cook the gyoza as per the directions on pages 60–61.

Kara-age

唐揚げ

(Japanese Fried Chicken)

No izakaya menu or Japanese cooking repertoire is complete without a solid kara-age recipe (pronounced "kah-rah-ah-gay"). I make mine in the Oita style, which is a little spicier and more garlicky than typical recipes. Kara-age uses only the thigh; people often ask me how I get my chicken so juicy—there's no secret. Just use the thigh and the bird does the work for you!

Yield:
2–4 servings

Ingredients:
2 cloves garlic
½ shallot
¼ oz (5g) fresh ginger
½ tbsp hot chili powder
½ tsp white pepper
2 tbsp soy sauce
4 tbsp sake (or mirin)
1 tsp sesame oil
2 tsp yuzu juice
2 tsp rice vinegar
2 boneless chicken thighs
vegetable oil, for deep-frying
10 tbsp (100g) potato flour (or rice flour or cornstarch)
¼ lime or lemon per serving
soy sauce or mayonnaise (optional)

Grate the garlic, shallot and ginger. Combine with the chili powder, pepper, soy sauce, sake, sesame oil, yuzu juice and vinegar in a bowl. Lay the chicken thighs out flat and cut them into quarters. Place the chicken pieces in a bowl, pour the marinade over them and refrigerate for at least 2 hours or preferably overnight.

Heat the vegetable oil to 325°F in a large heavy saucepan. Drain the chicken pieces in a sieve, then dredge each piece in the potato flour, laying them out in a single layer on a plate after dredging. Let them sit for a little while, then dredge the pieces again, shaking off the excess potato flour—the double dredging is to make sure all the moisture on the surface of the chicken is absorbed and covered, resulting in a crisper, less greasy chicken.

Line a plate or baking sheet with paper towels. Fry the chicken pieces in batches for about 5 minutes, or until deeply browned, then drain on the paper towels. Serve with a wedge of lime or lemon, and perhaps some soy sauce or mayonnaise.

Satsuma-age
さつま揚げ

(Fried Fish Cakes)

Legend has it that the ambitious Shimazu clan of Satsuma (present-day Kagoshima) brought this dish back from Okinawa after an excursion there in the 19th century. Thereafter it became more associated with Satsuma than with Okinawa and took on its current name, which literally means "Satsuma fry." Think of them as Japanese fish fingers, but . . . different. The fish itself is made into a forcemeat and then fried without breading, giving it an unusual but pleasant texture that is at once light, tender, chewy and crunchy. Bits of vegetables studded throughout add pleasant variation. Very good with sake or shochu.

Yield:

2 servings

Ingredients:

10½ oz (300g) (prepared weight) white fish fillet (use whatever fish you like, but since this dish is about 90% fish, use something flavorful and high-quality; I usually use really fresh lemon sole or whiting)

½ tsp dashi powder

pinch white pepper

about 1 oz (25g) frozen edamame (soybeans—not the ones in the shells)

½ carrot, cut into 4 long, thin planks

vegetable oil, for frying

Cut the fish into chunks and place in a food processor with the dashi powder and white pepper. Process to a smooth paste. (Alternatively, you can do this by chopping by hand or bashing it in a mortar for a more rustic texture.) If you wish, force the mixture through a sieve—this is an arduous process but it results in a more refined and, arguably, more authentic finished product.

Divide the mixture into 2 equal parts. Mix half of it together with the edamame, so the beans are evenly distributed throughout the paste. Rub your hands with a little oil, then shape the mixture into 4 oblong patties, kind of like a squashed football. Take the remaining mixture and wrap it around each of the carrot planks so they are completely covered (apply more oil to your hands if they start to get sticky).

Heat the oil to 325°F in a large heavy saucepan. Use a pair of tongs to lower each piece into the oil and cook for about 6–8 minutes, until the fish cakes are a deep golden color. Drain on paper towels and serve with tartar sauce or ponzu (pages 26–27).

Mackerel Scotch Egg, Obi-ten Style

鯖のスコッチエッグ飫肥天スタイル

(Mackerel Scotch Egg with Pickled Ginger Tartar Sauce)

The exact origins of tempura as we know it are mysterious—the word, as well as the dish itself, came from the Portuguese, but what the original dish was like is hard to say. However, at least two different dishes in the 16th and 17th centuries were described as tempura: one breaded, fried and simmered, and one battered and fried. But in all likelihood, there were more than two recipes that took the name "tempura" in early modern Japan.

One of these early tempuras may have been *Obi-ten*, short for "Obi tempura" and named for the town of Obi in Miyazaki, where it comes from. It is indeed deep-fried, but it isn't battered like modern tempura. Instead it resembles satsuma-age (pages 66–67) and is based on minced oily fish—usually mackerel or sardines. The tofu here gives a texture the Japanese call *fuwa fuwa*, meaning "fluffy and soft," like a marshmallow. So essentially, this is a deep-fried fish marshmallow. Or something. The miso and ginger spruce up the mackerel, while the starch binds and helps form a crisp crust.

These are a really, really exquisite snack with beer or shochu. You can also use tea-pickled eggs (pages 160–161) in place of plain boiled eggs.

Yield:
2 Scotch eggs

Ingredients:
For the pickled ginger tartar sauce:
2 tbsp mayonnaise
1 tsp hot English or Japanese mustard, or more to taste
¼ onion, finely chopped
½ oz (15g) beni shōga, finely chopped

For the Scotch eggs:
2 mackerel fillets, skinned and boned (about 5⅓ oz [150g])
¼ oz (5g) fresh ginger, finely chopped
1 tbsp (15g) miso
1½ oz (40g) firm silken tofu, pressed or microwaved to extract moisture
2 tbsp (20g) potato flour or cornstarch
pinch white pepper
vegetable oil, for deep-frying, plus extra for greasing hands
2 eggs, medium boiled (cooked a little longer than for tea-pickled eggs, pages 160–161)
salt or MSG, to taste

For the pickled ginger tartar sauce:
Stir all the ingredients together until combined. Set aside.

For the Scotch eggs:
Purée the mackerel, ginger, miso, tofu, potato flour or cornstarch and pepper in a food processor until it is very smooth. If you really want this to be super refined (or super authentic), force this mixture through a sieve with a spatula. But this is a Scotch egg, folks. No need to be that fancy. Refrigerate this mixture for at least 30 minutes to firm up.

Heat the vegetable oil to 350°F in a large heavy saucepan. Keep a small dish of vegetable oil nearby. Use this to lubricate your hands as the mixture is sticky. Enclose each egg in a handful of mackerel mixture, then drop each Scotch egg carefully into the oil as you make them. Fry the eggs for about 5–6 minutes—they should look quite brown, more an old bronze color than a bright gold. Drain on paper towels and season with a little salt while hot. Serve with the pickled ginger tartar sauce.

Unfortunately you can't really form these ahead of time because the mixture is too fluid and they won't hold their shape. (They're made using scoops or molds in Japan.) However, if you have to make a lot of them and time is an issue, you can par-fry them at a lower temperature, about 250°F, until barely golden, then let them cool and fry them later at 350°F until completely browned.

These are delicious hot, straight from the pan or at room temperature.

Nadōfu
菜豆腐

(Tofu Set with Vegetables)

Nadōfu is a kind of tofu set with vegetables. This is a pretty involved process, but I encourage you to try it—the end result is much more delicious than just about anything you can buy. If you want to make plain tofu, just omit the vegetables—the process is exactly the same.

Yield:
about 4 large servings, or 6 smaller ones

Ingredients:
10½ oz (300g) dried soybeans
3¾ qt (3.5L) water, plus ¾ cup (180ml)

Ingredients *continued*:
3¼ oz (90g) fresh vegetables
   (I often use 2 oz [60g] broccoli and
   1 oz [30g] carrots, for color)
1½ tsp (8g) salt
4 tsp (18g) Epsom salts or *nigari* (Japanese
   tofu salts)

Soak your beans in roughly 3 times their volume of water for at least 8 hours, preferably overnight. Drain and rinse the soaked beans. To make a soy milk, purée the beans in batches in a blender with some of the 3¾ qt (3.5L) water until very smooth (be mindful that the mixture will froth up and may overflow). Add the soy milk along with any remaining water to a large pan.

Bring the soy milk to a very gentle simmer. If you're a food science geek, you'll already know that soy lecithin is an excellent foaming agent. So unless your pan is really, really big, don't let the milk boil or you will have a lot of mopping up to do. Take it from me—I've made this mistake before.

Simmer the soy milk for about 15–20 minutes to cook out the beans' protein. The aroma will go from a starchy, grassy, raw green bean–like smell to a delightful, sweet, cake-batter smell. While your milk is simmering, prepare your vegetables. All the vegetables will cook in the soy milk at the same time, so cut them into small pieces, bearing in mind their respective cooking times—I do the carrots on a mandoline so they're quite thin, and separate the broccoli florets from their stalks, which I then split down the middle and cut into small chunks. The vegetables should end up very tender but not soft.

Line a colander with muslin and perch it over a large container. Ladle the soy milk into it. When the dripping slows, work it with a spatula. Eventually you'll end up with a fibrous pulp. Keep pressing down on this pulp to extract the milk, or, if it's not too hot, bundle the muslin around it and squeeze it out like a sponge. The resulting dry matter is called *okara*, and it's actually quite useful and really healthy, with tons of fiber and protein. Check the Internet for ideas on what to do with it; it freezes well if you haven't got an immediate use for it.

Pour the strained soy milk back into the pan and add the vegetables and salt. Bring it back to a simmer and cook until the vegetables are just tender (they will carry on cooking in the hot tofu as it cools). Stir the Epsom salts or nigari into ¾ cup (180ml) water until it dissolves completely. Add this solution to the soy milk and stir, then let it sit for a good 3–4 minutes to let the proteins coagulate.

To drain your tofu, you can use a colander or a perforated tray, or better yet, a tofu press. It's a pretty arcane piece, but if you plan to make a lot of tofu, it's invaluable. Line your press/colander/tray with muslin and perch it over another container to catch the whey as it drips. Scoop out the coagulated soy curds and vegetables with a slotted spoon. Tilt and gently shake the spoon to drain off excess liquid, then place the curds and any vegetables into your press. Carry on doing this until you've separated all the curds. At some point you'll want to switch to a sieve for this job, as the globules get smaller and smaller.

At this point, you could just gently drain the curds, dish them out, and enjoy them with a splash of soy sauce or ponzu tsuyu (pages 96–97) and some sesame seeds—this is one of my absolute favorite ways to have tofu. Still warm, loose and creamy, it simply melts in your mouth like a delightfully delicate cheesy custard, but far lighter and cleaner. But if you want firmer tofu, or you're saving it for later, weight down the curds with a plate, lid, board or another container so that all the extra moisture is pressed out.

After 1 hour, your tofu should be just firm enough to remove from the press and slice. If you want it even firmer, leave it in the press for another hour.

The tofu will keep in the fridge for a few days, or you can pack it in brine and let it ferment, in which case it can last many months. Serve the nadōfu cold with a simple sumiso sauce (pages 24–25), or you can use it however you'd generally use tofu.

Hitomoji Guru-guru

一文字ぐるぐる

(Scallion Bundles)

I must say, part of my affection for this dish is its ridiculous name. It could just be called "bundled scallions," but instead it's more fancifully described as *hitomoji guru-guru*, which translates roughly as "wound up to look like the character for the numeral 1." Silly. Anyway, these are from Kumamoto, where they're usually served as part of a larger lunch. I like to serve them as canapés, or as a sort of mini salad alongside richer dishes.

Yield:
4 tiny salads or canapés for 8

Ingredients:
2 bunches good-quality scallions,
    washed and trimmed of outer layers
    and roots
salt, to taste
about ¼ cup (60ml) sumiso (pages 24–25)

Prepare an ice bath or a bowl of very cold water. Bring a pan of salted water to the boil and blanch the scallions in batches for about 30–60 seconds, until pliable—you need to be able to wind the green part easily around the white part. Place them in the ice bath/cold water as soon as they're blanched, then drain in a colander.

Tip them out onto paper towels or a clean tea towel, then take the green end and bend it over, winding it tightly around the white end. To secure the bundle, just give it a squeeze. They should be about 2 inches (5cm) long—bite size; if your scallions are really long, you might have to fold them over twice or double up on the winding. Refrigerate in an airtight container, covered with a damp paper towel, until ready to serve. Don't keep them in the fridge for more than a few hours or they will lose their color.

You can either plate these up with the sumiso alongside as a dip or portion them out, pile them up and spoon a little sumiso directly on top.

Karashi Renkon

辛子レンコン

(Lotus Root Stuffed with Hot Mustard)

Lotus root is an ingredient so tasty and so cool to look at that I always wonder why it doesn't turn up on more restaurant menus. The aroma is similar to corn, but it's got a delicious flavor like a hybrid of water chestnuts, Jerusalem artichokes and peanuts. Plus, it has an otherworldly, incomparable appearance—one guest I served it to assumed it was some kind of cheese (even though it doesn't taste like cheese at all), bemused by its wide holes and pale flesh. When selecting lotus root (available from Asian markets), try to choose one that is at least 2 inches (5cm) in diameter and has an even width across its entire length.

This dish is synonymous with Kumamoto, ubiquitous at izakaya and souvenir stands around the prefecture. It's sweet with miso yet intense with mustard, a great dish to enjoy between sips of shochu.

Yield:	Ingredients:
2–4 servings	10½–12 oz (300–350g) lotus root (1 segment about 4¾ inches [12cm] long)
	2 tbsp vinegar
	4 tbsp (70g) white or mixed miso
	3¼ tbsp (50g) hot English mustard
	2 tsp all-purpose flour, plus ½ cup (60g) for the batter and more for dredging
	1 tsp sugar
	oil, for deep-frying
	½ tsp turmeric (optional)
	½ cup (120ml) sparkling water

Wash the lotus root, then cut the ends off and peel it. Cover with water in a saucepan, add the vinegar (to prevent the root from oxidizing and turning a weird red color) and boil for about 30 minutes—it should be tender all the way through when pierced with a skewer or fork. Drain and leave to cool.

Combine the miso, mustard, 2 tsp flour and the sugar into a smooth paste. Use a spatula to spread the filling out on a small plate or tray. Now stamp the lotus root into it, forcing the paste up through the tubes. Keep doing this until all the holes are completely filled. Wipe any excess filling from the outside of the root clean with paper towels.

Heat the oil in a large heavy saucepan to 320°F—as lotus roots are quite fat, it's best to use a deep, narrow pan rather than a wide, shallow one. Whisk the ½ cup (60g) flour and the turmeric (if using) into the sparkling water, to form a loose, airy batter. Dredge the stuffed lotus root in flour, dip it into the batter using a fork or a couple of skewers, then carefully lower into the hot oil. Cook for 5–6 minutes; you want to preserve the bright golden-yellow color of the batter so it matches the stuffing inside; don't let it get too dark. The batter is more for aesthetics than texture or flavor, anyway. Drain on a rack or paper towels and cool to room temperature. To serve, cut into slices just shy of ⅜ inch (1cm) thick.

Basashi

馬刺

(Horse Sashimi)

This is a "must-try" dish for visitors to Kumamoto, so iconic that it would have felt wrong to omit it from this book, even though it is, admittedly, quite weird. It is possible to source horsemeat in the UK, but it's a much more complicated matter in the US, where cultural resistance to the idea of it is even stronger. So if you're not keen to try horse, or can't get it—both very understandable—I've found that venison makes an excellent substitute. Plus, on my most recent trip back to Japan, I discovered that raw venison (called *shikasashi*) is actually a specialty of the remote island of Yakushima, so there is a precedent for it in Japan. Like venison, horse is a very lean meat, and it tends to become tough and dry when cooked beyond very rare. So although this dish may seem strange, I actually think it's one of the best ways to have horse or venison. I wasn't sure about it at first, but after just a few times eating it, I came to love it.

Yield:
2–4 servings

Ingredients:
7 oz (200g) horse rump or loin
½ onion
⅓ oz (10g) fresh ginger, grated
⅓ oz (10g) daikon, grated
4 leaves shiso, cut into chiffonade
soy sauce, to taste

Trim the horsemeat of all sinew and gristle, then place in the freezer for 30–45 minutes to firm up. Meanwhile, slice the onion thinly and place in a bowl of very cold water for 15 minutes or so, then drain. Combine the ginger and daikon and place a little mound of this mixture in your dipping bowls.

Slice the horsemeat very thinly across the grain, into roughly bite-size pieces. Serve alongside the sliced onion and shiso, and pour a little soy sauce into your bowls with the ginger and daikon. To eat, stir the ginger and daikon into the soy sauce, then pick up some onion and shiso along with a slice of horse, dip and enjoy. Fantastic with shochu.

Hiyajiru

冷や汁

(Chilled Miso Soup)

One of my all-time favorite dishes on a hot day. Some may find the idea of a cold miso and fish soup strange, but keep in mind all the cold miso and fish dishes found throughout Japan—this just takes those flavors and translates them into a refreshing liquid format. Usually this is served with a side of hot rice, so diners can enjoy the contrasting temperatures. I use room-temperature rice so everything stays nice and cold, but do whatever you prefer.

In Miyazaki this is dished up with a few ice cubes in it to keep it cold. I don't really like this because as they melt, they dilute the soup. To add flavor where it would otherwise be lost, I use cucumber-chili ice cubes, which make the dish both lighter and more exciting as you get to the bottom of the bowl. This will make more ice cubes than you need, but they are fantastic in a Bloody Mary or gin and tonic.

Yield:
4–6 servings

Ingredients:
For the cucumber-chili ice cubes:
½ cucumber
juice of ½ lime
2 Thai green chilies
2 tbsp (30ml) rice vinegar
3¼ tbsp (50ml) water
pinch salt

For the miso soup:
2 mackerel fillets or 4 sardine fillets
    (about 5⅓ oz [150g] total),
    skinned and boned
salt
1¾ tbsp (30g) miso
1½ tbsp (15g) toasted sesame seeds
2½ tbsp (40ml) rice vinegar
2½ tbsp (40ml) mirin
1¼ cups (300ml) dashi
¾ lb (340g) firm silken tofu, pressed to
    extract moisture
1½ cups (300g) rice
½ cucumber
¾ oz (20g) beni shōga, chopped
4 leaves shiso, cut into chiffonade
few drops of sesame oil

For the cucumber-chili ice cubes:
Simply purée all the ingredients in a blender. Pass the purée through a fine sieve and transfer to an ice cube tray. Freeze until set.

For the miso soup:
Season the fish with a little salt and broil until done—it should actually be a little overcooked so it's quite dry. Purée this in a blender along with the miso, sesame seeds, vinegar, mirin, dashi and 3½ oz (100g) of the tofu until completely smooth. Pass through a fine sieve into a container and refrigerate for at least 1 hour to get it really nice and cold. (The mixture will separate as it chills. Not to worry—store it in a jar and give it a good shake to bring it back together before serving.)

To serve:
Cook the rice. Cut the cucumber lengthwise, then shave it thinly—use a mandoline, if you have one. In a colander, salt the cucumber slices liberally and leave them to sit for 10 minutes, then squeeze out the liquid and give them a quick rinse under cold water. Cut the remaining tofu into small cubes. Place a mound of tofu and cucumbers in each bowl. Add a small spoonful of beni shōga on top, and then a pile of shiso chiffonade. Pour in the chilled soup, stopping just before it reaches the top of the tofu and cucumbers. Add a few drops of sesame oil and the ice cubes. Serve the rice on the side.

Tonjiru

豚汁

(Pulled Pork Miso Soup)

This is not a strictly southern dish, but it fits in very well with Kyushu's culture of porky comfort food. Essentially, this is an ordinary miso soup, bulked up and given extra depth and richness from the addition of pork ribs and hearty root vegetables. This is simple, inexpensive and crowd-pleasing; I first discovered it as a school-lunch item served in the winter at one of the schools where I worked. Satisfying as either a side or a main.

Yield:

4–6 small servings or 2–3 large servings

Ingredients:

1 rack pork spare ribs or baby back ribs
½ onion
2 cloves garlic
⅓ oz (10g) fresh ginger
1 qt (1L) dashi
¼ burdock root (available from Chinese supermarkets), washed and peeled
3½ oz (100g) turnips or rutabaga, peeled
1 large carrot, peeled
3¼ oz (90g) daikon, peeled
3 tbsp (55g) miso
1 Chinese chive or scallion, finely chopped
1 tsp sesame seeds
rāyu (pages 30–31) (optional)

In a large saucepan simmer the ribs, onion, garlic and ginger in the dashi for about 2 hours, until the meat is just starting to fall off the bone. Skim any scum off the surface and top up with water as needed. Meanwhile, cut the burdock and the turnips into thin shavings (use a vegetable peeler or a mandoline), the carrot into wedges and the daikon into semicircles about ⅛ inch (3mm) thick. Remove the ribs and strain the broth through a sieve into a clean saucepan.

When the ribs are cool enough to handle, strip the meat from the bone and tear into chunks—discard any stringy or tough cartilaginous bits.

Boil the carrots, burdock and turnips in the dashi-pork broth along with the miso until tender, then add the sliced daikon and cook for another 3–4 minutes until soft. Finally, add the pulled pork chunks. Serve in deep bowls and garnish with the Chinese chive or scallion, sesame seeds and rāyu (if using).

Kanimeshi
かに飯
(Crab Rice)

The water in Kyushu is as varied as its terrain—from the salty Pacific coast of Miyazaki and the mudflats of the Ariake Sea, to Kirishima's sulfuric hot springs and the fresh streams of Aso. This means that Kyushu's aquatic fauna are also very diverse, but perhaps none more than its prized crabs. One of them is Miyazaki's striking *asahigani*, literally "rising sun crab," so named for its almost circular body that turns bright red when cooked and looks a bit like the Japanese flag when placed on a bed of rice. This particular recipe comes from Saga, famed for its crab—particularly mitten crabs, similar to the velvet crabs found in Scotland or blue swimmer crabs found around the world. I use the frozen swimmer crabs found at Chinese supermarkets, but really this will work with just about any crab you can get your hands on. If you're not keen on picking fresh crab or can't get it, not to worry: pre-picked crabmeat will do as well.

I love the simplicity of this dish—aside from seasonings, it's got only two ingredients. The shells and dark meat of the crab impart their briny umami to the rice, which is flecked with sweet and meaty bits of its flesh. It's a lovely side, and the leftovers make wicked fried rice or yaki-onigiri (pages 146–147).

Yield:	Ingredients:
4–8 servings	12–14 oz (350–400g) whole crab, or
	3½–5⅓ oz (100–150g) picked crabmeat
	2⅓ cups (450g) rice
	2⅓ cups (540ml) water
	1 tbsp soy sauce
	1 tsp mirin
	1 tsp rice vinegar
	1 tsp sea salt or MSG
	1 small piece (about ¼–⅓ oz [5–10g])
	kombu, rinsed

Clean the crab or have your fishmonger do it for you: brush its shell clean, then remove the triangular abdomen flap, crack open its shell and remove the gray gills—these are nasty. (If you buy frozen swimmer crab, they usually come cleaned already, so you can skip this step.)

Rinse the rice 4 or 5 times, until the water is clear enough that you can see the individual grains through it. Cover with the water and leave to hydrate for 15 minutes.

Add the soy sauce, mirin, rice vinegar and salt to the rice, and top with the kombu and the crab. Bring to the boil, then cover and reduce the heat to as low as possible. Steam for 20 minutes, then remove the crab and discard the kombu. Pick all the meat from the crab and then fold it back into the rice. Save some of the crab claws for presentation.

Large Dishes
メインディッシュ

Mentaiko Pasta

明太子パスタ

One of the most popular uses for mentaiko is as an unlikely but delicious flavoring for pasta. Its salty, fishy, spicy edge complements a creamy, carbonara-like sauce, garnished with seaweed and a squeeze of lemon. If this all sounds a bit strange, consider *bottarga*—the dried, cured mullet roe enjoyed in northern Italy as a garnish for all manner of pasta dishes.

Yield:
2 servings

Ingredients:
2½–3½ oz (75–100g) karashi mentaiko
    (pages 50–51)
2 tbsp heavy cream
1 egg
2 tbsp (½ oz) Parmesan, grated
white pepper, to taste
chili powder, to taste
1 tbsp (15g) butter
1 clove garlic, finely chopped
5⅓–7 oz (150–200g) capellini, spaghetti
    or linguine
½ lemon
pinch aonoriko (green seaweed flakes)
    or shredded nori, to garnish
pinch black sesame seeds, to garnish
1 scallion, thinly sliced, to garnish

Cut open the mentaiko lobes and scrape out the eggs. I find the easiest way to do this is to slit them open lengthwise and press them through a sieve into a bowl. Discard the skins. Beat this together with the cream, egg, cheese, pepper and chili powder.

Melt the butter in a large frying pan and sauté the garlic gently until soft and mellow. Cook the pasta al dente and drain, then add it to the garlic and butter. Remove from the heat, and stir in the mentaiko-cream mixture (the residual heat from the hot pasta will cook the egg and thicken the sauce). Finish with a squeeze of lemon before dishing up. Garnish with aonoriko, sesame seeds and scallions.

Gōyā Champloo
ゴーヤーチャンプルー

(Bitter Melon, Tofu and Spam Stir-fry)

This simple stir-fry combines three ingredients that are often unpleasant on their own—bitter melon, Spam and tofu—and by some inscrutable Okinawan alchemy transforms them into a delicious, palatable comfort food. Bitter melon, also called bitter gourd or gōyā in Japanese, is a remarkable ingredient if only because it's amazing that anybody ever thought to eat it. In its raw state, it is so intensely, soapily bitter that whoever decided to cook with it must have been very desperate indeed. Or else they were just very confused, and thought it was a sort of lumpy cucumber. But despite its inherent harshness, it is very popular in China and in Okinawa, where one local microbrewery has even harnessed its bitterness to brew beer. And when you cook with it, it works—pre-salting and cooking help to dissipate its intensity, but it never totally loses its bitterness. In the finished dish, it comes across as a sort of astringent heat, boosted by chili, countered by the fatty saltiness of Spam and lending piquancy to the creamy nothingness of tofu. The flavor of the gōyā when subdued and integrated with the other ingredients reminds me of green beans—which would probably make an adequate substitute. I've also done this with Brussels sprouts, which work brilliantly—they have a slight bitterness as well, although it's nowhere near what you get from gōyā.

As for the Spam, you don't have to use it—some recipes call for ham, some for bacon and some for thinly sliced pork in its place. But Spam is totally authentic; in many Pacific islands, it became a popular ingredient due to the gastrocultural influence of American GIs during World War II. And actually, I really like it—it has a great squidgy texture when cooked, and it's got a good, porky flavor. By the way, this is an excellent dish to have with beer—the bitterness of the gōyā and the saltiness of the Spam were simply made for a cold pale ale.

Yield:	Ingredients:
4 servings	1 large gōyā (bitter melon) (7–9 oz [200–250g])
	1 tsp salt
	about 7 oz (200g) Spam or ham
	3½–5⅓ oz (100–150g) firm tofu, excess water removed
	2 eggs
	1 tbsp soy sauce
	1 tbsp mirin
	pinch white pepper
	pinch chili powder or flakes, plus more to garnish
	vegetable oil, for stir-frying
	2 tsp sesame seeds

Prepare the gōyā by cutting the ends off, then slicing it in half lengthwise and scraping out the seeds and white pith with a spoon. Remove as much of the white part as you can, as it's the most bitter part, and it has a funny texture. Slice the gōyā into half rounds about ⅛ inch (3mm) thick and toss with the salt. Let it sit for about 20 minutes to leach out some of the bitterness, then rinse it under cold water for a minute or so to lessen the saltiness.

Cut the Spam into little chunks about ⅜–¾ inch (1–2cm) thick, a little smaller than bite-size. Do the same with the tofu. Beat the eggs together with the soy sauce, mirin, pepper and chili powder.

Heat the oil in a pan and add the Spam. Let it brown a bit, stirring occasionally, then add the gōyā. The gōyā should cook for about 5–6 minutes—you want it to retain its texture but cook off the bitterness. Add the beaten egg mixture and stir it in, and just before it's set, stir in the tofu—it's okay if the tofu breaks up. To serve, garnish with sesame seeds and a little chili powder. Serve with rice.

Yaki-curry
焼きカレー
(Curry Rice Gratin)

This dish, from the port city of Mojiko, is one of the first foods I mention when people ask what southern Japanese food is all about—it's spicy, it's rich, it's unrefined and it doesn't seem particularly Japanese at first glance. It sounds a bit like something a British student would make after an evening on cheap lager: steamed rice topped with curry and grated cheese. So wrong, yet so right.

I have no idea how this became a specialty of Mojiko—chances are one restaurant invented it, then others simply copied them. But I do know that Mojiko is the port where the banana first entered Japan, so I incorporate it into my curry sauce. Banana adds a pleasant fruity sweetness in the background, but you can leave it out if you prefer. In fact, this dish works fine with basic Japanese curry sauce, and you can use just about any vegetables you like. You can add meat too, but as it is, this makes a great vegetarian main.

Yield:
4–6 servings

Ingredients:
For the curry sauce:
7 oz (200g) Japanese curry roux
1 qt (1L) water or vegetable stock
1 very ripe banana (about 3½ oz [100g])
3¼ tbsp (50ml) soy sauce
1 tbsp yuzu juice
1 tbsp hot chili sauce (or more or less, to taste)
1 tbsp curry powder
4½ tbsp (65g) butter
½ oz (15g) dark chocolate

For the yaki-curry:
1½ cups (300g) Japanese rice
1⅝ cups (375ml) water
3–4 carrots, peeled
14 oz (400g) potatoes, peeled
10½ oz (300g) cauliflower
1 tbsp vegetable oil
1 large onion, chopped
1 quantity of curry sauce
3½ oz (100g) mushrooms
about 2¾ oz (80g) Cheddar cheese, grated
about 2¾ oz (80g) mozzarella cheese, grated
4–6 onsen eggs (pages 54–55) or soft-boiled eggs, 1 per serving

For the curry sauce:
Put the curry roux with the water or stock in a pan and stir until the roux has dissolved. Bring to the boil. Add all the other sauce ingredients, stir and remove from the heat. Use an immersion blender to purée everything together.

For the yaki-curry:
Preheat the oven to 425°F. Cook the rice according to the instructions on pages 42–44.

Cut the vegetables into bite-size pieces, bearing in mind their cooking times—the carrots and potatoes take longer to cook than the cauliflower, so cut the cauliflower a bit larger. Heat the oil in a large saucepan, add the onion and cook over a medium heat until it just starts to color. Add the rest of the vegetables except the mushrooms, then add the curry sauce and bring to the boil. Cook until the vegetables are tender, stirring the sauce frequently to ensure nothing sticks. Add the mushrooms at the end of the cooking time so they retain their bite.

Lightly grease a casserole dish or baking sheet. Add the cooked rice and spread it in an even layer on the bottom. Ladle the vegetable curry over, then top with the grated cheeses. Bake for about 10 minutes or until the cheese melts and just starts to brown.

To serve, dish the curry into shallow bowls and top each serving with an onsen egg.

Sara Udon
皿うどん

(Crispy Noodles with Vegetables and Seafood)

Japanese noodle terminology can be confusing. For example, *soba* usually means buckwheat noodles, but it can also mean egg noodles, as in yakisoba. In fact, when I first had yakisoba, I mistakenly thought the restaurant had made it wrong because they used ramen instead of actual soba. But udon pretty reliably refers to one thing, and that's thick, chewy wheat noodles. Except here. This dish uses very thin, crispy fried noodles. I have no idea how it got its name, which literally just means "plate udon," but it might have something to do with the fact that the rarely used *kanji* characters for *udon* are quite close to the Chinese characters for *wonton*, which may have been how the crispy noodles were originally described.

Anyway, it's essentially a Chinese-style stir-fry hailing from Nagasaki, dressed with a thickened stock. You've probably had some ancestral variant of it at a Cantonese restaurant, where it's likely to be called seafood noodles or something similar. It's got a lot of lovely textures, with just-cooked vegetables and seafood along with noodles that are half-crisp, half-soft on the plate. Like its soupy cousin chanpon (pages 178–179), it's always a mad jumble of ingredients, so feel free to change up the vegetables and seafood as you like—snap peas, bamboo shoots, nira and bok choy are all good options. The original version uses thinly sliced pork instead of bacon (deduct 10 authenticity points), but bacon is always an upgrade.

This dish doesn't call for any seasoning; there's usually enough from the broth. But have soy sauce or salt at the ready if you find it lacking.

Yield:
4 servings

Ingredients:
For the sauce:
⅞ cup (200ml) chicken stock
⅞ cup (200ml) dashi
2 tsp mirin
2 tsp vinegar
1 tbsp cornstarch mixed with a little cold water

For the sara udon:
4 bacon strips
vegetable oil
3½ oz (100g) squid rings
3½ oz (100g) shrimp

Ingredients *continued*:
3½ oz (100g) scallops
1 large onion, cut into ⅛-inch (3mm)-thick slices
1 hot chili (optional), thinly sliced
1 carrot, peeled and sliced into long planks
1¾ oz (50g) shiitake or other mushrooms
¼ cabbage, cut into ¾-inch (2cm) chunks
3½ oz (100g) bean sprouts
⅓ oz (10g) fresh ginger, peeled and julienned
2 tsp sesame oil
5½–7 oz (160–200g) crispy fried noodles (if you can't find these, cook and drain ramen, then fry them in oil until hard and golden)
sesame seeds, to garnish
black pepper, to taste

For the sauce:
Boil the stock, dashi, mirin and vinegar in a small pan and let it reduce by about a third. Stir in the cornstarch slurry, a little at a time, until it thickens. It should be like gravy, not like glue—don't go overboard. Keep the sauce at a low simmer until needed.

For the sara udon:
Fry the bacon in a tiny bit of oil in a frying pan or wok until brown and crisp, then drain on paper towels. Crank up the heat, then cook the squid rings, shrimp and scallops separately in the bacon grease. The heat should be very high, and don't crowd the pan so that everything develops a nice color without overcooking. The squid tubes and shrimp should only take about 1 minute on each side; the scallops 2 minutes on each side. If your scallops are large, turn down the heat and cook them for about 3–4 minutes on each side. Put the cooked seafood to one side. Add a little more oil to the pan, if necessary, turn up the heat again, add the onion and cook for about 3 minutes. Add the chili (if using) and carrot and cook for another 2–3 minutes, then add the mushrooms, cabbage, bean sprouts and ginger. Cook for another 3 minutes or so, then stir in the sesame oil and the cooked seafood. Keep everything really hot.

To serve, put the noodles in a bowl and crush them into smaller pieces with your hands—they should be about 2 inches (5cm) long. Put some of the crushed noodles on each dinner plate, arranging them like a flattened bird's nest. Pile the stir-fry in the center of the noodles (making sure everybody gets a scallop!), then pour on the sauce; it should cover the seafood and vegetables but leave most of the noodles dry. These will get stirred into the rest of the dish by the diners, giving them a pleasant contrast of crispy and soft noodles that will change as they eat. Garnish with sesame seeds and season with lots of black pepper.

Yaki-udon

焼きうどん

(Stir-fried Udon Noodles)

I just enjoyed a wokful of this recipe, and it was so good, it made me wonder why it isn't more popular than yakisoba, the dish on which it is based. They're essentially the same thing—stir-fried noodles with loads of veggies in a sweet-salty sauce—but the fat, chewy, toothsome texture of the udon is, I think, far more satisfying than the egg noodles you get in yakisoba.

Though this dish does turn up on lunch menus around Japan, it's considered a specialty of Kitakyushu, the city where I lived in Japan. I don't know why, though it might be because it's at a crossroads of mainstream Japanese food culture (featuring more traditional noodles like udon) and Kyushu food culture (which has more Chinese-inflected noodle dishes, like ramen and yakisoba). Anyway, it's delicious and easily made in about half an hour.

Yield:
2–3 servings, depending on your appetite

Ingredients:
1–2 tbsp vegetable oil
1 small or ½ large onion, sliced about ¹⁄₁₆ inch (2mm) thick
4 bacon strips, cut into small chunks, or 2 oz (60g) lardons (optional)
1 carrot, cut on the bias into thin planks
1 clove garlic, julienned
½ cabbage (use a pointy or flat cabbage if you can get it, cut into strips about ⅜ inch [1cm] wide)
7 oz (200g) bean sprouts

Ingredients *continued*:
2¾ oz (80g) mushrooms, sliced
1 tbsp sesame oil
½ tsp dashi powder or MSG
½ tsp white pepper
1½ tbsp soy sauce
1 tbsp mirin
½ tbsp rice vinegar
2–3 portions cooked udon noodles
1½ oz (40g) beni shōga (drained weight)
white sesame seeds, to garnish
crispy fried shallots, to garnish (optional)—you can buy these in Asian markets or big supermarkets

Heat the oil until very hot in a wok or deep frying pan. Add the onion and bacon (if using) and stir-fry until just starting to brown, then add the carrot and cook for another 1–2 minutes. Add the garlic, cabbage and bean sprouts and stir-fry for another 3–4 minutes, until the cabbage has lost much of its volume. Add the mushrooms and stir, then add the sesame oil, dashi powder, pepper, soy sauce, mirin and vinegar. Stir, then add the udon and cook for another 2 minutes or so, until the noodles are warmed through and much of the liquid has been absorbed.

To serve, pile the stir-fry into shallow bowls and top each serving with a mound of beni shōga, some sesame seeds and a handful of crispy shallots (if using).

Variations:
Instead of the soy-sauce-mirin-vinegar blend, you can use store-bought yakisoba sauce or katsu sauce (pages 28–29), which is tangy and sweet, similar to a thick Worcestershire sauce. You can also make this with shellfish: big shrimp, squid rings and scallops are typical. Add them toward the end of cooking so they aren't overcooked.

Tempura
天ぷら

(Fried Seafood and Vegetables with Ponzu Tsuyu)

When people ask me to suggest a simple but authentic Japanese recipe they can work into their culinary repertoire, tempura is usually my response. It's easy, it's delicious, and it can be made with ordinary cupboard ingredients—nothing more exotic than soy sauce.

Tempura is an izakaya staple beloved throughout Japan, but its origins lie in Kyushu. We know it comes from the Portuguese, but beyond that we can't be sure what the first tempura was like; some early recipes actually describe a dish similar to nanban-zuke (pages 104–105). But this recipe is for tempura in its modern form, with the lightest of batters providing a crunchy enclosure in which the contents essentially steam in their own moisture. This is more a technique than an actual recipe—the specific ingredients I leave up to you. It's a fantastic way to make the most of super-fresh seasonal vegetables and fish, and also a great way to use up odds and ends of vegetables left in the fridge. We've all been stuck with a third of an eggplant or four lonely asparagus spears and not known what to do with them. Tempura is the answer.

Yield:
4 servings

Ingredients:
For the ponzu tsuyu:
6½ tbsp (100ml) dashi
6½ tbsp (100ml) ponzu (pages 26–27)

For the tempura:
10½–14 oz (300–400g) fresh vegetables—
  asparagus, zucchini, broccoli, mushrooms,
  onion and squash are some of my favorites
14–17½ oz (400–500g) boneless and
  skinless white fish fillets (sole, plaice, whiting,
  pollock, cod, etc.), or 8 large raw jumbo
  shrimp, shelled and deveined
vegetable oil, for deep-frying
2¼ cups (500ml) cold sparkling water
1 egg
scant 1¾ cups (220g) all-purpose flour
pinch salt

To serve:
3½ oz (100g) daikon, peeled and
  finely grated

For the ponzu tsuyu:
Mix together the dashi and ponzu and set aside.

For the tempura:
Prepare the vegetables by cutting them into pieces that will cook quickly, bearing in mind that some vegetables cook faster than others. For example, leave asparagus whole, but cut onions into thick slices and squash into thin slices. Cut the fish fillets into 1¼-inch (3cm) strips.

Heat your oil to 350°F in a deep, wide saucepan, wok or deep-fryer. While it's coming up to temperature, make the batter. Combine the sparkling water, egg, flour and salt in a bowl and whisk until it is the consistency of heavy cream. Don't overmix—small lumps are good as they will cause the batter to puff up and become light. It is also important to make the batter just before frying, so that the bubbles remain in the mixture and it stays cold. This will help create a light, delicately crunchy texture without excess oil. If you don't have a thermometer, you can test the temperature by dropping a little batter into the oil—if it sinks and doesn't rise, it's too cold; if it immediately floats and starts to brown, it's too hot; if it sinks for a moment and then floats, it's perfect.

Dredge the vegetables in the batter and fry for just 3–4 minutes, until the batter is a light golden brown. Drain on a wire rack. Repeat this process with the fish or shrimp. Don't crowd the pan as this will cause the tempura to stick together and lower the temperature of the oil.

Tempura is best eaten fresh out of the fryer—ideally, you should eat everything as soon as they come out, then go back and fry some more. However, you can also keep them hot and crisp in an oven set to about 225°F with the door open slightly to let out any moisture. Just don't stack them.

To serve:
Give everyone a little dish of ponzu tsuyu and a small mound of grated daikon and place the tempura in the center of the table. Enjoy with your hands or with chopsticks. A bowl of rice will complete the meal.

Toriten

とり天

(Chicken Tempura)

Toriten is one of Kyushu's several famous fried chicken recipes, originating in Oita. Chicken isn't a typical tempura ingredient in most of Japan, but I love the contrast of crisp batter and juicy meat.

Yield:

2–4 servings

Ingredients:

2 boneless, skinless chicken breasts
salt
white pepper
tempura batter (pages 96–97)
vegetable oil, for deep-frying
ponzu tsuyu (pages 96–97)
¼ lemon, cut into wedges

Slice the chicken into ⅜-inch (1cm)-thick pieces and season with salt and white pepper. Dredge the chicken in the batter and cook following the method for the tempura recipe on pages 96–97. Serve with ponzu tsuyu and a wedge of lemon.

Chicken Nanban

チキン南蛮

(Fried Marinated Chicken with Vinegar Sauce and Tartar Sauce)

Chicken nanban is a specialty of Miyazaki prefecture and a classic example of what is called *yōshoku*—Japanized Western food. It combines a strange array of Portuguese, British and Japanese influences into one of the most mouthwatering chicken dishes in Japan—hell, in the world! This is a crunchy, juicy, sweet-and-sour chicken explosion served with creamy, zesty tartar sauce. My version uses quite a lot of fresh ginger in the marinade to make the whole dish really sing.

Yield:
4 servings

Ingredients:
For the chicken and the vinegar sauce:
⅝ cup (150ml) rice vinegar
⅓ cup (75ml) mirin
3 tbsp (35g) sugar
3½ oz (100g) fresh ginger (peeled weight), roughly chopped
pinch salt
pinch white pepper
3¼ tbsp (50ml) soy sauce
5 tsp (25ml) Worcestershire sauce
1½ tbsp (25g) ketchup
4 boneless, skinless chicken breasts

For the tartar sauce:
3 tbsp (35g) gherkins or cornichons
3⅓ tbsp (50g) mayonnaise
1 egg, hard-boiled

Ingredients *continued*:
2 scallions, roughly chopped
4–5 sprigs parsley, roughly chopped
¼ tsp dried dill
2 tsp (10g) yellow mustard
½ tbsp (10g) white miso
1 tsp rice vinegar
1 tsp sugar
pinch salt

For the batter:
vegetable oil, for deep-frying
3 eggs
1½ cups (210g) all-purpose flour
½ tsp baking soda
1 cup (270ml) water
white pepper
salt

To serve:
¼ cabbage, finely shredded

For the chicken and the vinegar sauce:
Purée all the ingredients except the chicken in a blender until completely smooth. Pass through a fine sieve to remove any fibrous ginger bits. Cut the chicken into chunks or strips about ¾ inch (2cm) thick. (Alternatively, you can pound the chicken to a thickness of about ¾ inch [2cm]; the main thing to bear in mind is that it needs to be thin enough to cook quickly in the oil.) Pour the marinade over the chicken pieces in a container and stir to coat the chicken evenly. Cover and refrigerate for 2–8 hours. Remove the chicken, pour the marinade into a saucepan and boil for a few minutes. Pass the sauce through a fine sieve and keep in the fridge until needed.

For the tartar sauce:
Chop the gherkins into fine dice. Place all the remaining ingredients in a blender and purée until smooth. Stir in the diced gherkins.

For the batter:
Heat the oil to 350°F in a large frying pan. Whisk together all the other ingredients in a bowl to form a smooth batter. Pat the surface of the chicken with paper towels to ensure that it's quite dry, then dredge in batter and fry for 6–8 minutes, until a rich golden brown. Drain on paper towels.

To serve:
Place the chicken on a bed of shredded cabbage and top with the tartar sauce. Serve the reserved vinegar sauce on the side in a small dish or ramekin. Serve with rice or potato salad.

Tonkotsu

とんこつ

(Sweet Pork-Rib Stew)

The word *tonkotsu* (pork bones) usually refers to ramen, but in Kagoshima it can also refer to this dish, a hearty, stripped-back, sweet pork-rib stew. This is proper comfort food, almost like something that could have come out of Ireland or France, except for the distinctly southern Japanese flavors: soy sauce, shochu, miso and brown sugar. Many recipes for tonkotsu call for *konnyaku*, a flavorless jelly made from a starchy Japanese root vegetable. Add it if you wish (it's got no calories, so it's good for diets), but you will definitely not be missing out if you don't. If you like tonkotsu, you may also want to try tonjiru (pages 80–81), a less sweet, soupier cousin.

Yield:
2–4 servings

Ingredients:
1 rack (14–17½ oz [400–500g]) pork loin
    ribs (baby back ribs)
1 tbsp vegetable oil
3¼ tbsp (50ml) shochu (or you can use rum,
    which works very well indeed)
2 tbsp soy sauce
1 tbsp rice vinegar
1 tbsp mirin
water, to cover (about 1½ cups [350ml])
2 tbsp brown sugar
2 tbsp miso
½ oz (15g) fresh ginger, sliced
5⅓–7oz (150–200g) konnyaku, cut into
    bite-size slices or cubes (optional)
2–3 carrots, cut into bite-size wedges
about 7 oz (200g) daikon (or potatoes), cut
    into bite-size half rounds
pickles, like beni shōga, kimchi (pages
    32–33) or takana-zuke (pages 166–167)

Use a sharp knife to separate the ribs. Heat the oil in a deep casserole dish and fry the ribs on all sides until nicely browned—do this in batches so the ribs don't steam in each other's juices. Remove the ribs from the pan and add the shochu, scraping up the bits on the bottom with a wooden spoon. Put the ribs back into the pan, then add the soy sauce, rice vinegar, mirin and enough water to cover the ribs. Add the brown sugar, miso, ginger and konnyaku (if using) and give everything a stir. Bring to a low simmer and cook for about 1½ hours, maybe 2. The rib meat should be barely hanging onto the bones. (Ask yourself: could I eat this with chopsticks? If the answer's no, cook for a little longer.)

Remove the ribs and discard the ginger (the konnyaku can stay in the liquid; it won't overcook). By this point, the liquid should have reduced by about half so it's nice and thick; if it hasn't, bring the liquid to the boil and reduce to a gravy-like consistency. Add the carrots and daikon to the broth and cook on a medium simmer for about 10–15 minutes, or until quite tender. Return the ribs to the broth. Serve in deep bowls with rice and pickles.

Nanban-zuke

南蛮漬け

(Japanese Escabeche)

One of the original "nanban" dishes prominently features two ingredients that would have been considered identifying hallmarks of barbarian European cookery in the 16th century: vinegar and peppers. *Zuke* means pickled or marinated, and, traditionally, this calls for a double marinade: first, the raw fish is semi-cured in a vinegary marinade, and then after breading and frying the fish, it's placed back in the cooked and thickened liquid so the coating can reabsorb the flavors. I don't really like this—it tends to make the breading go soft, and isn't the whole point (or at least the main point) of deep-frying to create a satisfying crunch? You really get enough flavor from the first marination and from serving the sauce with the fish anyway. Just bear in mind that this recipe is not 100% authentic—but it is 100% delicious. If you don't feel like deep-frying, shallow-frying works pretty well, too.

Yield:

4 servings

Ingredients:

9 tbsp (130ml) rice vinegar
6½ tbsp (100ml) dashi
2 tbsp mirin
2 tbsp soy sauce
1 tbsp sugar
1 tsp hot chili powder, or 2–3 whole dried red chilies, chopped

Ingredients *continued*:

4 fillets (14–17½ oz [400–500g]) meaty but lean fish—red mullet, sea bass or bream works well—scaled (leave the skin on) and pin bones removed
vegetable oil, for deep-frying
1 green pepper, thinly sliced
1 onion, thinly sliced
2 tsp potato flour or cornstarch
1 tbsp water
all-purpose flour, for dredging
sesame seeds, to garnish
hot chili flakes, to garnish

Stir together the vinegar, dashi, mirin, soy sauce, sugar and chili until the sugar is dissolved. If your fish fillets are very large, cut them into strips no wider than 1½ inches (4cm). Pour the marinade over the fish and marinate for 1–2 hours.

Heat the oil to 375°F in a large heavy saucepan. Remove the fish from the marinade, drain the marinade into a saucepan and add the green pepper and onion. Stir together the potato flour and water to create a thin paste. Boil the green pepper and onion in the marinade until just tender, then stir in the potato-flour mixture to thicken.

Pat the fish dry with paper towels, then dredge in all-purpose flour, leave it to sit for a bit and then dredge it again to ensure there are no wet patches on the surface. (Wet is the enemy of crisp.) Fry the fish for 3–5 minutes until golden brown, then drain on paper towels.

To serve, place some green pepper and onion in a shallow bowl and pour over a little of the sauce. Place the fish on top of the vegetables. Garnish with sesame seeds and chili flakes and serve with rice.

Mizutaki

水炊き

(Chicken Hot Pot)

This Fukuoka specialty is essentially Japanese chicken soup, a light but hearty one-pot dish full of vegetables, chicken thighs and steamy broth. It's part of a category of dishes called *nabemono*, or one-pot foods, that are often prepared in the kitchen but finished at the table by the diners themselves—vegetables are added just before they're eaten so they maintain their color and texture. If you've got a little portable gas burner and a sturdy pot, I encourage you to try the communal cooking style yourself—it's a lot of fun, especially with plenty of cold sake, beer or shochu to contrast the piping hot soup.

In terms of vegetables, you can add almost anything you like to the mizutaki—there aren't many rules. I also love this with some cooked *tsukune* (pages 134–135) dropped in.

Yield:
4 servings

Ingredients:
6–8 chicken thighs, skinless, boneless and trimmed of cartilage and excess fat
about 5 cups (1.2L) chicken broth, dashi or (ideally) a mixture of both
⅓–½ oz (10–15g) fresh ginger
about 21 oz (600g, 4 portions) fresh udon or ramen noodles, or about 10½ oz (300g) dried *harusame* (glass noodles)
8–10 shiitake or chestnut mushrooms, stems removed

Ingredients *continued*:
3½ oz (100g) enoki or beech mushrooms
4 leeks, trimmed of outer green leaves and cut into 1-inch (2.5cm) chunks on the bias
2 carrots, thinly sliced
½ whole Chinese cabbage, sliced into 1¼–1½-inch (3–4cm) square chunks
3½ oz (100g) snow peas
about 7 oz (200g) aromatic, leafy greens—spinach, shiso, chrysanthemum greens, mustard greens, mizuna (Japanese mustard greens) and Chinese broccoli work well
2 scallions, thinly sliced
1¾–2 oz (50–60g) daikon, grated (optional)
⅞ cup (200ml) ponzu (pages 26–27)

For the broth:
Cut the chicken thighs into bite-size pieces and put them in a saucepan with the chicken stock and/or dashi and the ginger. Bring to a simmer, skimming off any scum that forms on the surface. Simmer gently for about 15 minutes. Remove from the heat, take out the chicken and set aside. Discard the ginger.

If you're cooking everything in the kitchen:
Bring a pan of water to the boil and add the noodles; cook for 1–3 minutes, until al dente, then drain and rinse under cold water. Add the mushrooms to the broth and cook until just tender, then add the leeks and cook for another minute or so. Add the carrots, Chinese cabbage and snow peas and cook until just tender, then add the greens and let them wilt. Divide the noodles and chicken between deep bowls, then ladle in some broth and vegetables. Garnish with scallions and daikon (if using). Serve with ponzu, which can be used for dipping or mixed directly into the soup.

If you're cooking at the table:
Bring the prepared vegetables, cooked chicken and uncooked noodles to the table on platters. Put a little ponzu, scallions and grated daikon (if using) into each deep bowl at the table. Bring the pot of broth to the table and set it on a gas burner on a medium heat. Bring to a simmer, then allow everyone to pick their own vegetables and chicken from the platters and cook to their liking, dipping them in ponzu before eating. At the end of the meal, add the noodles to the broth and cook until al dente, then divide the broth and noodles into each bowl; the remaining ponzu will season the broth and noodles.

Motsu Nabe

もつ鍋

(Offal Hot Pot)

And the winner of "least popular recipe" goes to . . .

It would be amiss to omit this recipe from the book, as it's such an important star in the Fukuoka culinary constellation. And yet I expect almost no one to cook it. Why? Because it boldly features chitterlings—stinky, chewy chitterlings. Now, I like chitterlings, but it was definitely an acquired taste for me, and I totally understand why many people don't like it. It smells and has the texture of what it is: an animal poo delivery tube. If you've ever had French andouillette sausage, you already know that reeks like something you probably shouldn't be eating. As if that weren't enough of a hurdle to trying this, they're also hard to get—I tried almost every butcher I know before resorting to an Asian market's freezer, where you can find it under the amusing label "pig fat end."

However, if you're one of those people who really loves tripe, or if you're keen to acquire the taste, then you're in for a real treat. I first had this dish without knowing exactly what it was, probably to my benefit. I found it rich and tasty, if a little smelly and chewy. But one thing that's great about it is that it is piled with a melange of other powerfully flavorful ingredients to match the chitterlings' musk: raw garlic and chilies, nira and miso. The end result is something far more pleasant than entrails ought to be—it'll always be a little funky, but the seasonings create an enticing perfume. If you make this, then you get a bonus 1,000 authenticity points. You're a real Fukuoka local now.

Yield:

4 servings

Ingredients:

14–16 oz (400–450g) chitterlings
(pig intestines)
2 tbsp sake or shochu
salt
about 3⅓ cups (800ml) water
3 tbsp (50g) miso
1–2 tbsp hot chili sauce (optional)
1 tbsp mirin

Ingredients *continued*:

2 tsp rice vinegar
½ oz (15g) fresh ginger, peeled and thinly
sliced
¼ cabbage, chopped
5⅓ oz (150g) bean sprouts
4 portions thick ramen noodles,
or cooked rice
6–8 nira, cut into ¾–1¼-inch (2–3cm) pieces
2 fresh red chilies, thinly sliced
2–3 cloves garlic, thinly sliced
kimchi (pages 32–33)

Cut the chitterlings into roughly bite-size pieces. Place in a large saucepan, cover with water and add the sake or shochu and a good pinch of salt, then bring to the boil. Take off the heat and discard the water—this will cleanse the intestines and take away some of their stink.

There are two ways of cooking this dish. Fast is more traditional, but I think slow is tastier—the tripe is more tender, and the resultant broth is exquisitely rich.

If you're cooking it fast, bring about 3⅓ cups (800ml) water to a simmer in a heavy pan, then whisk in the miso, chili sauce (if using), mirin, vinegar and ginger. Have your blanched intestines and all your vegetables ready to go. First put the intestines in and let it cook for just a minute or two, then add the cabbage and bean sprouts. Let them cook for 2–3 minutes until just slightly soft. If you're using noodles, add them to the broth now, then kill the heat and scatter the nira, chilies and garlic on top. If you're using rice, serve it on the side along with the kimchi. If you're preparing it this way, you can also do it at the table, using the same instructions for mizutaki (pages 106–107).

If you're cooking this slow, add the blanched chitterlings back to the pan along with the miso, chili sauce (if using), mirin, vinegar and ginger, and cover with water. Bring to a simmer and put a lid on it, and let it cook for about 1–2 hours, checking periodically to top up with water. Taste the chitterlings; they should be tender rather than rubbery, but still with a bit of chew. When it's to your liking, add the cabbage and bean sprouts and cook for 2–3 minutes. If you're using noodles, add them to the broth now, then kill the heat and scatter the nira, chilies and garlic on top. If you're using rice, serve it on the side along with the kimchi. Now go open a window, because your house probably smells like a barn.

Tonkatsu

豚カツ

(Pork Schnitzel)

Tonkatsu, not to be confused with tonkotsu (pages 102–103), are Japanese pork cutlets, breaded and deep-fried. The word is a conjunction of *ton* (pork) and *katsu*, short for *katsuretto* (cutlet). So there you have it. It's a simple dish, popular throughout Japan, but especially in Kyushu. Kagoshima in particular is famous for its luxurious *kurobuta* ("black pigs"), a breed whose ancestors are the prized British Berkshire pigs. They make excellent schnitzel. Actually, they make excellent everything.

A quirky Kumamoto variation of this recipe uses horse, a local favorite more commonly eaten raw (see basashi, pages 76–77). It's really quite delicious—if you try it, just make sure it's still rare in the middle or it can become tough and dry.

Yield:	Ingredients:
4 servings	1⅛–1⅓ lb (500–600g) good-quality boneless pork loin chops or horse strip loin or fillet
	1 tsp white pepper
	⅔ cup (80g) all-purpose flour
	3 eggs, beaten
	1⅓ cups (80g) panko bread crumbs
	oil, for frying
	sea salt, to taste
	6½ tbsp (100ml) katsu sauce (pages 28–29)
	½ cabbage (napa cabbage is best), finely shredded
	splash rice vinegar or umezu (plum vinegar)

Lay the pork chops between 2 sheets of plastic wrap, and bash the hell out of them. You can use a meat mallet, a rolling pin or any other heavy, blunt object for this. Flatten them out to no thicker than ⅜ inch (1cm). Mix the white pepper into the flour. Dredge the cutlets in the flour, then the beaten egg, then the panko, ensuring they are evenly and densely coated.

Heat about ⅜ inch (1cm) oil in a wide frying pan— it shouldn't be smoking, but it should be very hot. Test the temperature by flicking a little egg into the oil; it should immediately start sizzling and floating but not browning too quickly. Fry the cutlets for 2–3 minutes on each side and drain on a wire rack. Season with sea salt as soon as they come out of the oil. Let the cutlets rest for 5 minutes or so before slicing into bite-size chunks. Drizzle with katsu sauce and serve with cabbage dressed with a little vinegar and some rice alongside.

Simmered Sole

クチゾコの赤酒煮

In the Ariake Sea there is a kind of flatfish known as *kuchizoko* in the local Saga prefecture dialect. Interestingly, this translates directly as "foot sole," and indeed, it's very similar to the sole found around the coast of England, with a pleasantly firm texture and sweet flavor. And chefs in Saga agree with their European counterparts that it's best cooked on the bone, which helps prevent overcooking and also contributes more flavor to the flesh.

But there the similarities end. Instead of frying or baking with, say, brown butter and capers, in Saga the fish is usually simmered, or poached, in a thin sauce featuring a sweet, funky cooking sake called *akazake*—"red liquor." Kagoshima and Kumamoto are the main areas of akazake production, but even there it's an unpopular drink—I don't think I ever encountered it at bars or restaurants. It's more common to find akazake in recipes like this one—it adds an almost malt-like sweetness and a hint of beet earthiness to the fish. Combined with soy sauce, vinegar and umeboshi, it gives the finished dish a sweet-and-sour character, which, in a way, isn't that far off what you get from capers and brown butter.

One thing: you can't get akazake outside of Japan, at least not as far as I'm aware. But the common Chinese cooking liquor known as Shaoxing wine makes an excellent substitute, especially cut with a little mirin to lighten it up. Alternatively, you can just use mirin.

Yield:

2 servings

Ingredients:

⅜ cup (90ml) dashi

2 tbsp (30ml) soy sauce

1 tbsp (15ml) mirin

2 tbsp (30ml) Shaoxing wine (or use more mirin, or even sherry)

1 tsp sugar

2 tbsp umeboshi purée or vinegar—use brown rice vinegar or umezu (plum vinegar) if you can

1 whole Dover or lemon sole (or a small plaice or similar flatfish), cleaned and outer frilly fins cut off

pinch sanshō, to garnish

pickled ginger

greens

Stir together the dashi, soy sauce, mirin, Shaoxing wine, sugar and umeboshi/vinegar in a pan large enough to fit the fish. Bring to the boil and reduce slightly, stirring to make sure all the sugar and umeboshi has dissolved.

Reduce the heat to a very low simmer and add the fish. Cook for about 3–4 minutes, then carefully turn the fish over (use tongs and a spatula for support) and cook for another 3–4 minutes. The fish should pull away easily from the bone when done.

Remove the fish and gently peel off the skin on both sides, then transfer to a shallow bowl or deep plate for serving. Pass the simmering liquid through a sieve and pour a little over the fish. Garnish with a pinch of sanshō. Serve with pickled ginger, greens, rice and steamed vegetables or a salad.

Taco Rice

タコライス

An American, a Mexican and an Okinawan walk into a bar . . .

This dish sounds like a bad ethnic joke: distinctly Okinawan comfort food based on an American military preparation of a dish originating in Mexico. It's weird by almost anyone's standards—not the Japanese, not the Americans and certainly not the Mexicans would claim it as their own. But despite its dubious ancestry, this dish can only call one place home, and that's Okinawa. It's another strange—but delicious—by-product of the US military's presence there, originally invented by a local cafe owner named Matsuzo Gibo in the 1980s. Once a favorite among GIs, it's now a staple of school cafeterias, homestyle restaurants and fast-food chains around southern Japan. To give this a Japanese flavor, you'll find some typical Japanese spices here, but you can replace them with more traditional, authentic Tex-Mex ingredients like cumin or chipotle chili. Of course, authenticity should be just about the last thing on your mind when you're making something as culturally amorphous as taco rice. Make it your own, with whatever flavors you enjoy.

Yield:
4 servings

Ingredients:
1–2 tbsp vegetable oil
17½ oz (500g) ground beef
1 large onion, chopped
2 cloves garlic, chopped
¼ tsp white pepper
1 tsp mild chili powder or paprika
1 tsp hot chili powder
1 tsp shichimi (or more hot chili powder, plus the zest of 1 orange)
1 tsp sanshō or ground Szechuan pepper

Ingredients *continued*:
17½ oz (500g) tomato purée, or
　14 oz (400g) can of tomatoes
2 tbsp soy sauce
1 tsp mirin
1 tbsp yuzu juice or the juice of 1 lime
salt, to taste
4 portions cooked rice
2¾–3½ oz (80–100g) Cheddar cheese, grated
pickled jalapeños, radishes, kimchi, hot salsa or other topping (optional, to taste)
2 heads Little Gem lettuce, cut into quarters lengthwise

Heat the oil on high heat in a large frying pan and add the ground beef. Fry without stirring for 4–5 minutes, until it has formed a nice brown crust on one side. Turn over and brown the other side, then remove from the pan. Reduce the heat slightly and sauté the onion until soft, using the moisture from it to scrape any bits of meat off the bottom of the pan. Add the garlic and cook for another 3–4 minutes, then stir in all the spices and let them cook out into the oil for 1–2 minutes.

Return the ground beef to the pan and break it up, stirring it into the onion and spices. Pour in the tomato purée, soy sauce, mirin and yuzu or lime juice. Stir well, cover and reduce the heat to low. Leave to stew for 30–60 minutes and then season with salt. Serve on the cooked rice, topped with cheese and pickles (if using), with the lettuce on the side.

Variation:
This is really delicious using braised beef instead of ground beef. Use about 21 oz (600g) ox cheek, beef shin or brisket, cut into cubes, and follow the method opposite, but instead of cooking it on the stovetop, cover it and cook in the oven set to 250°F for about 6 hours. When the beef is very soft, pull it apart it with a fork and work it into the gravy.

Rice Yaki

ライス焼き

(Fried Rice and Cabbage Pancake)

This obscure dish, most likely invented at an izakaya called Takobō in Kumamoto, is Kyushu's answer to okonomiyaki. If you've not had okonomiyaki, you should—I know only one person who doesn't like it, and he's weird. It's associated mostly with Osaka, where it's essentially a cabbage pancake topped with a sweet sauce and filled with all sorts of ingredient combinations (okonomi means "as you like"). In Hiroshima, the pancake becomes a thin crepe that tops a pile of cabbage and fried noodles. The Kumamoto version is sort of like the Osaka version, but it's filled with rice. Think of it like a big disk of fried rice with a lovely crispy crust on the bottom, like Persian tahdig. In keeping with okonomiyaki customs, you can add pretty much anything you fancy to this—like curry powder, corn, bean sprouts or kimchi.

Yield:
3 pancakes

Ingredients:
1 cup (200g) rice
4¼ oz (120g) cabbage, sliced
3 scallions, thinly sliced
1¾ oz (50g) scallops, chopped up
if they're big
1¾ oz (50g) squid, cut into small squares
1¾ oz (50g) shrimp, roughly chopped
pinch white pepper

Ingredients continued:
1½ oz (40g) mozzarella or similar cheese,
cut into small cubes
3 eggs
½ cup (65g) all-purpose flour
vegetable oil, for frying
6 bacon strips, cut in half
4 tbsp okonomi sauce or katsu sauce
(pages 28–29)
Japanese mayonnaise (optional)
3 pinches katsuobushi (optional)
aonoriko (green seaweed flakes, optional)

Cook the rice as you would normally (see pages 42–44), maybe a little firmer than usual as it will continue to steam as the pancake cooks. Let it cool to room temperature, then mix together with the cabbage, scallions, scallops, squid, shrimp, white pepper, cheese, eggs and flour. You may want to use your hands to break up any clumps of rice.

Unless you've got a very large griddle, you will likely have to make one pancake at a time. Heat a generous glug of oil in a frying pan or griddle (you'll need a good layer of it to keep the rice from sticking), then cook one-third of the bacon until just starting to brown.

Pour a third of the pancake mixture over the bacon in the pan, using a spatula to help form it into a disk. Cook on one side for about 5 minutes, keeping your eye on the heat—it should not be too hot so the pancake doesn't burn. Now here's the tricky part. Flip the pancake over—this is a two-spatula job, and you'll want to make sure the entire base is loosened from the pan before attempting to flip. Alternatively, you can slide your spatula underneath the pancake to release it, then turn it over into another oiled frying pan. Cook for another 5 minutes or so. In the last 2 minutes of cooking, spread the okonomi or katsu sauce all over the surface of the pancake, making sure it goes all the way to the edge. Carefully lift out the pancake onto a heatproof plate and keep it hot in a warmed oven while you prepare the rest of the pancakes.

To serve, carefully transfer the pancakes onto warmed dinner plates (again, use two spatulas). Squeeze a spiral or a zigzag of mayonnaise over the sauce if you like. Garnish with a big pinch of katsuobushi and a sprinkling of aonoriko if you want.

The Sasebo Burger
佐世保バーガー

That's right—there's a Kyushu city famous for that most un-Japanese food, the classic American burger. The city of Sasebo in Nagasaki prefecture is home to a US naval base, so burger businesses have boomed there in response to officers' big American appetites. Your typical Sasebo burger is pretty basic in terms of flavors, known instead for its long list of toppings and generous girth. But my ramped-up version features bold Kyushu flavors, including various ramen elements like chāshū and māyu.

Yield:
4 burgers

Ingredients
For the pickled onions:
3¼ tbsp (50ml) boiling water
1 tsp salt
3 tsp sugar
¼ oz (5g) kombu (about 4-square-inch [10cm] piece)
1 red chili, cut in half
6½ tbsp (100ml) rice vinegar
2 tbsp mirin
1 onion, thinly sliced

For the māyu mayo:
1 egg yolk
½ tbsp (10g) miso (preferably Hatchō miso)
⅝ cup (150ml) black māyu (page 30)
pinch white pepper

For the Sasebo sauce:
1½ oz (40g) gherkins, diced
¾ oz (20g) capers, finely chopped
⅓ oz (10g) chives, thinly sliced
2 tsp rice vinegar
2⅓ tbsp (30g) mayonnaise
2 tbsp (40g) gochujang or spicy miso butter (page 170), or 2 tbsp (40g) miso mixed with 1 tbsp chili powder
1 tbsp (15g) English mustard

For the burgers:
4 large sesame burger buns or rolls
¼ head iceberg lettuce, roughly torn
2 tomatoes, sliced no thicker than 3/16 inch (5mm)
4 shiitake mushrooms, chopped
1¾ lb (800g) good-quality ground beef, nothing too lean
sea salt and pepper
vegetable oil, for frying
4 eggs
8 slices burger cheese
8 portions cola-braised chāshū (pages 162–163), reheated

For the pickled onions:
Pour the boiling water over the salt, sugar, kombu and chili in a bowl. Stir to dissolve the sugar and salt, then set aside for 10–15 minutes to infuse. Add the rice vinegar and mirin, stir and add the onion slices—pack them in to make sure they're submerged. Refrigerate for at least an hour, or ideally overnight.

For the māyu mayo:
Whisk together the egg yolk and the miso until it forms a smooth paste. Slowly drizzle in the māyu, drop by drop at first, whisking constantly. Keep drizzling and whisking until completely emulsified. If it splits, put another egg yolk and a splash of warm water in a clean bowl and drizzle in the broken mayo, whisking constantly. Finish by stirring in the pepper and set aside.

For the Sasebo sauce:
Stir everything together until it looks like burger sauce. (If you're using the spicy miso butter, it will have to be at room temperature or slightly melted.)

For the burgers:
Slice your buns and toast 'em. I do this under the broiler, cut side up, so that the outside stays soft. Smear their bottom halves with a spoonful of māyu mayo. Add a pile of lettuce and then 2 or 3 slices of tomato. Mix the shiitake into the ground beef, then form into big, floppy patties no thicker than ¾ inch (2cm) and season well. Cook them on a hot griddle or in a frying pan over very high heat with a little vegetable oil for about 7 minutes, flipping every minute, for a medium-rare burger. Temperatures and patty thicknesses vary, so go with your instincts (an underdone burger can be saved by more cooking; an overdone burger is a hopeless disaster).

While the burgers are cooking, fry the eggs in a separate pan. Time it so that the eggs are ready just before the burgers, and you can place the cheese on the burgers and help it melt by topping it with warm chāshū and a hot egg. Transfer the stack to the bottom bun. Top with a handful of pickled onions and a dollop of Sasebo sauce. Top with the other bun, give the whole thing a good squish, then get in there and get messy.

Grilled Items

焼き物

Kushiyaki

串焼き

(Stuff on a Stick)

In Kitakyushu, one of the go-to gorging houses for me and my fellow expats was a place called Yakyū-dori, a kushiyaki shop run by a baseball-obsessed man (*yakyū* means "baseball") whom we simply knew as Master. Master loved foreigners—and we found in his premises a haven to be our boisterous selves. He liked to flirt with the girls and set up the guys with Japanese women. He would send huge amounts of delicious kushiyaki (skewered items) to our table along with all the cheap lager and umeshu we could drink, sometimes taking a break from the grill to join us in a beer or two. There was an effortlessness about him, both in his unpretentious, enthusiastic demeanor and in his cooking, which was always unbelievably delicious.

Kushiyaki isn't a strictly southern food, but it is one of my fondest food memories of Kyushu. The recipes here are quite like what you'd find at Yakyū-dori. Use bamboo skewers that have been soaked in water so they don't burn on the grill; you can also wrap the ends in foil to protect them. The best way to make these is on a very hot outdoor grill, with a few bricks stacked onto it, spaced so that the ends of the skewers rest on them like a bridge, supporting the meat above the coals. But they're all tasty under the broiler as well.

If you're planning a kushiyaki meal, prepare about 6–8 skewers per diner, and serve alongside rice, pickles and a salad or bowls of miso soup. Please note that the quantities given here are for short Japanese-style skewers, which are about 4 inches (10cm), roughly half the length of your average wooden skewers.

Above: Master getting friendly with my now-wife, Laura, on a fairly typical Friday evening in Yakyū-dori.

Above: Master reaching for my colleague Simon's genitals with his cooking chopsticks—another fairly typical evening.

Pork Belly

豚バラ

Although I did eat these skewers at restaurants, I associate them mostly with Japanese summer festivals, which are always a bonanza of food on sticks, suitable for ambulatory eating—an otherwise rare behavior in Japanese society. In Britain we are more accustomed to eating pork belly that's been slow cooked—except, of course, when it comes to bacon. And that's what this is like: over the high heat of the grill it becomes beautifully brown and crisp in places, chewy in others. Be sure to season liberally with salt or MSG to enhance its naturally mouthwatering quality.

Yield:	Ingredients:
about 6 skewers	10½ oz (300g) pork belly, rind off
	6½ tbsp (100ml) mirin or shochu
	sea salt, dashi powder or MSG
	white pepper
	hot mustard and Japanese pickles,
	to serve (optional)
	½ lemon, cut into wedges, to serve

Slice the pork belly very thinly—about ¹/₁₆ inch (2mm) thick, ⅛ inch (3mm) at most. You may want to put it in the freezer for 30 minutes or so to firm up before you cut it. Cut the strips into chunks, about 1½ inches (4cm) square, and thread them onto skewers. Put them in a bowl with the mirin or shochu to marinate for about half an hour, then drain and season with lots of salt, dashi or MSG.

Broil or grill until really well browned; if cooking over gas or charcoal, have a water bottle handy to take care of flare-ups, because these will release a lot of fat. Remove the skewers and season with a light dusting of white pepper. Serve with mustard and pickles if you want and a wedge or two of lemon.

Bacon-wrapped Scallops
ホタテベーコン

Funnily enough, a pseudo-Japanese-Polynesian version of these called *rumaki* was a staple at family get-togethers when I was growing up. My uncle Erik made them, threaded on toothpicks and marinated in a mixture of soy sauce and red wine. Delicious. But then scallops and bacon are a no-brainer. Make more of these than you think you'll need—they will get eaten!

Yield:
about 5 skewers if your scallops are big;
10 if they're little

Ingredients:
10½ oz (300g) fresh scallops (keep the roe on if you like)
10–12 bacon strips
6½ tbsp (100ml) sake
black pepper or sanshō
½ lemon, cut into wedges, to serve

If your scallops are on the large size (¾–1 oz [20–30g] each), cut the bacon strips in half. If they're smaller, cut the bacon into thirds. Wrap the bacon around each scallop and secure it by threading it onto skewers; use 3 or 4 small ones or 2 big ones per skewer. Place in a shallow dish and pour the sake over them (top it up with a little more if they're not covered). Marinate in the fridge for about 30 minutes.

Remove the skewers from the sake and pat them dry on all sides with paper towels. Broil or grill them until the bacon is nicely browned—use a higher heat for small scallops so the bacon cooks quickly, without overcooking the scallops. Season with plenty of black pepper or sanshō and serve each portion with a lemon wedge.

Bacon-wrapped, Cheese-stuffed Padrón Peppers

チーズししとうベーコン

Japan has a variety of pepper called *shishitō* that looks a bit like jalapeños but tastes mild and sweet. You can occasionally get them here, and they're becoming easier to find in the US, but it's more common to find Spanish Padrón peppers, which are very close in size and flavor.

Yield:
about 4 skewers

Ingredients:
5⅓ oz (150g) Padrón peppers
3½ oz (100g) mild, firm cheese, such as mild
   Cheddar or Edam, grated
8 bacon strips, cut in half
shichimi tōgarashi, to taste

With a paring knife, slit the peppers down one side to open them up, making sure not to cut all the way through either end. Stuff each one with as much cheese as you can, being careful not to tear the pepper. Close the open side of the pepper and wrap each one in half a bacon strip, ensuring that the pepper is totally covered.

Thread the peppers onto two skewers (to keep them from spinning around) and broil or, better yet, grill them over screaming-hot coals. The peppers are done when the bacon is nicely browned/blackened. Sprinkle with shichimi and allow to cool slightly before serving.

Bacon-wrapped Vegetables

野菜ベーコン

Bacon isn't the first thing that comes to mind when most of us think of Japanese food, and yet you'd be hard-pressed to find a kushiyaki restaurant in Japan that doesn't use it, harnessing its inherent salty deliciousness to enhance chunks of fresh vegetables. The most common variety is *aspara-bacon*, using asparagus, but I use any vegetables that are fresh and in season, so long as they lend themselves well to the quick, hot cooking of the grill. Tough vegetables like carrots don't work so well; tender ones like zucchini are perfect.

Yield:
8–10 skewers

Ingredients:
7–10½ oz (200–300g) fresh vegetables
(asparagus, baby leeks or leek hearts,
sugar snap peas, Brussels sprouts, etc.)
10–12 bacon strips

Prepare the vegetables by cutting them into chunks or sticks (if necessary) about 1¼–1½ inches (3–4cm) long and ⅜–¾ inch (1–2cm) thick. Cut the bacon into thirds, and wrap each chunk of vegetable in a strip of bacon. Skewer them to secure. Broil or grill until the bacon is nicely browned with some blackened bits.

Beef with Hot Mustard
わがらし牛肉

Hot Japanese mustard's sinus-clearing punch is a natural choice for beef, like horseradish with a Sunday roast. So simple, yet so satisfying. I'm slightly ashamed to admit that I often surreptitiously snarfed more than my fair share of these from the communal kushiyaki platters Master served to us at Yakyū-dori. You can use good-quality boneless pork loin instead of beef—it's equally delicious cooked in this way.

Yield:
6 skewers

Ingredients:
1⅛ lb (500g) beef rump or 1⅛–1⅓ lb
(500–600g) good-quality boneless
pork loin
¼ cup (60g) hot English or Japanese mustard
2 tsp mirin (optional)
sea salt

Trim the beef of any sinew, then cut across the grain into slices 1⅜ inches (3.5cm) thick. Cut these into chunks roughly 1¼ inches (3cm) square. Thread them onto skewers using a weaving pattern, folding the beef onto itself as you go. Rub the beef with the mustard and season on both sides with sea salt. (If you're using Japanese mustard, mix it with the mirin to thin it.)

Broil or grill on a very high heat for about 4 minutes, until just cooked.

Chicken Livers with Umeboshi

梅干しレバ

I served this at a barbecue, and a bunch of people told me that they don't usually like chicken livers, but they liked this. So I knew I was onto a winner. The umeboshi purée has an intensely fruity, sweet-and-sour (mostly sour) flavor that offsets the metallic richness of the liver.

Yield:
5 skewers

Ingredients:
14 oz (400g) chicken livers
1 clove garlic
¼ oz (5g) fresh ginger
2 tbsp soy sauce
1 tbsp mirin or umeshu
1 tsp sesame oil
1 tbsp rice vinegar
1 tbsp umeboshi purée (*neri-ume*),
   plus more for serving
sesame seeds, to garnish (optional)

Trim the chicken livers into bite-size pieces and trim away any sinewy or discolored bits. Grate the garlic and ginger and combine with all the other ingredients except the sesame seeds. Marinate the livers in this mixture for 4–8 hours, stirring once to redistribute.

Thread the marinated livers onto skewers. Broil on high or grill until nicely blackened. Dot each piece of liver with a little extra dab of umeboshi purée. Garnish with sesame seeds.

Tsukune

つくね

(Chicken Patties)

Tsukune. Just the word makes my mouth water; it has a juicy, lip-smacking quality. They're just chicken meatballs or, maybe more accurately, chicken patties, but they're seasoned with garlic and ginger, and they're simply one of the most addictive yakitori items out there. You can have these by themselves, coated in tare (pages 24–25), dipped in ponzu (pages 26–27) or dropped into a simmering pot of mizutaki (pages 106–107).

You may find other recipes for this that call for using a food processor, or for the addition of cornstarch and eggs; all this is meant to yield a smoother, lighter end product. I say bah! to that. I love the toothsome texture of hand-minced chicken, and there's no need for filler here. But I certainly won't tell you not to use a food processor if you have one—just don't overprocess it to a chickeny mush.

Yield:

8 patties or 16 meatballs, 4 servings

Ingredients:

4 boneless, skinless chicken thighs,
    trimmed of cartilage
⅓ oz (10g) fresh ginger, grated or finely
    chopped
1 clove garlic, grated or finely chopped
big pinch white pepper
1 scallion or nira, chopped
big pinch salt or MSG
soy sauce tare (pages 24–25), to serve

Cut the chicken into small chunks, then mince it either with a cleaver or in a food processor. When there aren't any big chunks left (everything should be roughly smaller than ³⁄₁₆ inch [½ cm]), mix everything else except the soy sauce tare into the minced chicken and use your hands to shape into oblong patties (no thicker than ¾ inch [2cm]) or meatballs.

Thread them onto skewers and brush with soy sauce tare and broil or grill for about 4 minutes on each side. Or you can just heat a little oil in a pan and sauté for 4–5 minutes on each side, until cooked through and firm to the touch, with a nice brown crust on the outside. Finish with another brush of tare on each side just before they finish cooking.

Chicken Skin

鳥皮

Chicken skin is one of my most cherished vices. I wouldn't call it a guilty pleasure, because I don't feel the slightest bit of guilt when I eat it—only delirious ecstasy. All fat and crunch and flavor, but of course they're a little tricky to cook. The challenge is to render off the fat as much as possible so that there's no unpleasant squishiness, without overcooking or burning the exterior, which is difficult on an open flame, and harder still under a broiler. So I cheat slightly by par-frying the skins and then finishing under the broiler. You end up with crunchy-succulent "cracklings" with a lick of smoke and a slight char.

Yield:
4 skewers

Ingredients:
skin of 2 chicken breasts (about 3½ oz [100g])
vegetable oil, for frying
sea salt or MSG
sanshō

Cut the skin into strips about ¾ inch (2cm) wide. Skewer them by folding them over themselves into little bundles. Wrap the ends of the skewers in foil to protect them from spattering grease. Heat some oil in a pan to a moderate heat—you can use a deep-fryer for this, set to about 300°F, or just shallow-fry them. Lay or dip the skins in the oil—if you're shallow-frying, stand back, because they'll spit like a camel. (You may want to use a lid or a mesh splatter guard.) Cook for about 6 minutes, turning often.

Another option that's a little cleaner and healthier is to bake the skewered skins at 350°F for about 15 minutes—the fat will render off, and they'll be ready for the broiler or grill.

Once the skins are golden, drain them on paper towels. Finish them under the broiler or on the grill for another 5–6 minutes or so, until deep gold and browned in places. Season liberally with salt or MSG and sanshō. Devour between gulps of beer.

Buttered Garlic
にんにくのバター焼き

We don't often eat garlic on its own, but when cooked properly, it's gorgeous—one of my favorites at kushiyaki shops. The heat of the broiler soothes its sulfuric fury, assisted by our old friend butter.

Yield:
4–5 skewers

Ingredients:
2 bulbs garlic
4¼ tsp (20g) butter, melted
1 tbsp soy sauce

Peel all the garlic. Yes, it's annoying, but it's worth it. I find the easiest way to do this without smashing the cloves is to firmly grasp each one by its top and tail, and give it a twist between your fingers. With a little luck, the skin should loosen and come off easily. I've also seen a video on YouTube where this guy puts a bunch of garlic in a big metal bowl, caps it with another bowl, and shakes the hell out of it for about 10 seconds. The garlic comes out completely peeled. I don't know if it really works, but let me know if you try it. Anyway, thread the garlic onto skewers; use a twisting or screwing motion as you do this to drill rather than spear into the cloves, or they might split. Make a little tray out of aluminum foil that fits all the skewers. Pour the butter and soy sauce over them and broil until golden brown; the heat should be moderate so that the garlic mellows and softens before the outside gets too dark. Awesome with beer or whisky highballs.

Mushrooms with Spicy Miso Butter
辛みそバターきのこ

Oita prefecture has a lot of hot, humid forests, perfect for growing mushrooms, especially shiitake, which are often broiled and served very simply with salt. They are delicious, but of course that's contingent on getting really excellent, fresh shiitake. This recipe will work with just about any big, meaty mushroom, but my favorite is eringi. Also known as king oyster mushrooms, they are available from specialty markets and Asian supermarkets. They're huge and impressive (i.e., kinda phallic), and their flavor and texture are like a mix of button mushrooms, chicken breast and tofu: meaty, toothsome and satisfying. Combined with the fatty, spicy umami of the miso butter and the lovely burnt bits that come from the broiler, the overall flavor oddly reminds me of a mushroom and chorizo pizza.

Yield:
about 6 skewers

Ingredients:
5⅓ oz (150g) fresh shiitake, eringi,
    portobello or similar big, meaty mushrooms
2 tsp–1 tbsp (10–15g) spicy miso butter
    (page 170), at room temperature
½ lemon, cut into wedges, to serve

Cut your mushrooms, if necessary, into bite-size pieces (shiitake and others of a similar size can be left whole) and thread them onto skewers. Place on a lightly oiled baking sheet, cut side down, and broil for 4 minutes. Turn, spread each one with some spicy miso butter, and grill for another 5 minutes. Serve immediately with a wedge of lemon or two.

Iwashi Mentai

鰯明太

This is advanced-level fishiness for people who love intense seafood flavors. Fishy fish eggs stuffed into fishy fish. Amazing after a few glasses of shochu, this Fukuoka preparation will smack your palate into submission with its mixture of richness, salt and spice. You will need a really, really hot broiler to make this dish sing—you may consider employing a blowtorch to finish.

Yield:

4 sardines

Ingredients:

about 2¾–3½ oz (80–100g) karashi
    mentaiko (pages 50–51)
4 sardines, head, guts and scales removed
    but bones left in
salt
½ lemon, cut into wedges, to serve
chili powder or shichimi tōgarashi, to serve
    (optional)

Use a spatula or butter knife to spread the mentaiko into the sardine cavities; it should bulge out slightly. Season both sides with salt, then place under the broiler on a lightly oiled baking sheet or on the grill for about 3–4 minutes on each side. The skin should be slightly blackened and crackly; keep cooking the sardines until you achieve this color (don't worry about overcooking; sardines are very forgiving because they're so oily).

Serve piping hot with wedges of lemon and a sprinkle of chili powder or shichimi tōgarashi if you want. To eat, use chopsticks to gently pull the meat off the bone along with some of the mentaiko.

Miyazaki-style Grilled Chicken

宮崎風味地鶏炭火焼

This is a really easy but really delicious chicken dish from Miyazaki, where it is known as *jidori sumibiyaki*: "charcoal-grilled local chicken." Simple as that. It's got a light marinade, but it's all about quality meat—get something corn-fed, if you can. The chicken is cut into bite-size chunks and grilled over intense heat, sometimes in a basket placed directly on the coals. This makes it blacken deliciously while still maintaining a bouncy and succulent texture. If it's not grilling weather, this recipe works well in a frying pan or wok—let it get really smoking hot to achieve a similar char as you'd get from hot charcoal. You'll need a fine grill mesh or a vegetable basket for this recipe.

Yield:	Ingredients:
4 servings	4 boneless chicken legs
	2 tbsp soy sauce
	1 tsp yuzu-koshō (pages 16–17)
	2 tsp mirin
	2 tsp rice vinegar
	2 tsp yuzu juice
	2 tsp shochu or sake
	½ tsp sesame oil
	vegetable oil, for the grill
	14 oz (400g) bean sprouts
	salt
	black pepper
	1 tsp toasted sesame seeds
	2 scallions, thinly sliced

Cut the chicken into bite-size pieces. Combine the soy sauce, yuzu-koshō, mirin, vinegar, yuzu juice, shochu or sake and sesame oil, and pour over the chicken. Marinate for 8–24 hours.

Prepare your grill with the grate set as close to the heat as possible. Lightly oil the grate or grill basket, and when the fire is red hot, add the chicken. Keep the chicken moving with tongs—it's almost like stir-frying, but over a direct flame. Depending on the grill, it will take 5–10 minutes to cook through. Make sure the chicken has got some nice black bits on it.

While the chicken is cooking, season the bean sprouts with salt and pepper and grill them in a separate basket, or dry-fry them in a pan. To serve, place a bed of bean sprouts on a dish, and pile the chicken pieces on top. Garnish with sesame seeds and scallions. Yum yum. I'm getting really hungry writing this right now.

Yaki-onigiri
焼きおにぎり

(Grilled Rice Balls)

Onigiri are rice balls, often filled with something delicious, and they are a fundamental part of Japanese snacking—sort of like sandwiches in the UK and US. They are typically triangular but can be round or rectangular as well—the word *onigiri* simply means "squeezed," which is how they're made. You may notice it's the same word used to describe the kind of sushi that is just rice with fish on top: *nigiri-zushi*. Making them triangular takes a bit of practice, but for some reason I think they're just more fun that way.

Yaki-onigiri is onigiri that's been grilled or panfried, so it goes delightfully brown and crispy on the outside—think of the texture of rice crackers. These are a great stomach filler for a snacky izakaya meal, and also a great way to use up little scraps of ingredients or leftovers, like bits of Miyazaki grilled chicken or chāshū trimming, for the filling. Strong-flavored pickles and other preserved foods are popular fillings as well; umeboshi is the classic choice, but kimchi (pages 32–33), braised kombu (pages 34–35) and ume-shiso cucumber (pages 36–37) are some of my favorites.

Yield:
4 servings

Ingredients:
6½ oz (180g) rice (uncooked weight)
fillings of your choice (pages 32–37)

For the glaze:
3¼ tbsp (50ml) soy sauce
1 tsp sugar
4¼ tsp (20g) butter, melted

To serve:
oil, for grilling or frying
nori, cut into large strips or squares (optional)

For the onigiri:
Cook the rice (see pages 42–44) and spread it out on a plate to cool. Have a bowl of salted water on hand. Wet your hands to keep the rice from sticking, and grab a handful of rice, gently compressing it, using the joint between your thumb and index finger on your dominant hand to form the angular sides, and your other hand to press it into a sort of patty.

To add filling, press the rice between your palms to flatten it out, then add a spoonful of your filling into the center and wrap the rice up around it before shaping it. It's kind of like making a Scotch egg. One method I've seen to facilitate filling is to lay out a square of plastic wrap, then put down a layer of rice, then a spoonful of your filling in the middle, and enclose it by drawing up the corners of the plastic wrap. Then just unwrap, squeeze and shape.

For the glaze:
Stir all the ingredients together in a bowl until the sugar dissolves. Brush this mixture onto one surface of the onigiri, being careful not to use too much, as the moisture and the fat will cause the rice to fall apart.

To serve:
Grill, broil or sauté the onigiri with a small amount of oil on a medium heat for 3–4 minutes on the glazed side, then cook the other side, remembering to brush the other surface with more of the glaze before turning. When the surface is bubbly and bronze, brush with the glaze once again and finish cooking for about 30 seconds on each side. The most typical way of serving these is with a piece of nori, which you wrap around the onigiri to keep your hands from getting sticky, and to add umami. But it's not strictly necessary.

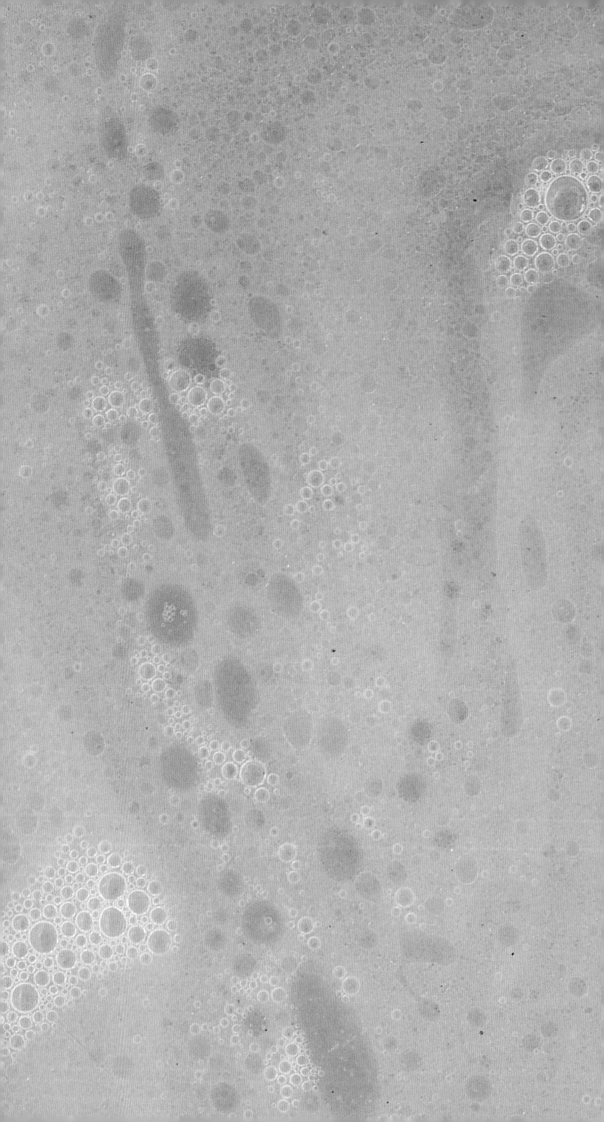

Ramen

ラーメン

The beauty of good ramen cannot be understated: noodles with the perfect bite, bathed in an indulgent broth that's been lovingly cooked for hours or days, in a bowl overflowing with toppings and texture and flavor . . . and then it's gone in a flash of fervent slurping, like cherry blossoms felled by a windy rain, leaving only a melancholy memory.

Is it too much to call it the world's most perfect food? It's a labor of love, it's a quick lunch, an indulgent dinner, a soothing hangover cure and an infinitely customizable expression of individuality, but still rich in history and tradition.

And despite its complexity, it's very doable for the home cook. It requires very little in the way of special or expensive ingredients—all it requires, really, is time and care. These recipes will show you how to build your ramen from the ground up, starting with the broths, then the noodles, then the toppings and, finally, fully formed preparations from around the south of Japan, and a couple of my own inventions. But once you know the basics, feel free to assemble them however you like—no two ramen shops are the same, and that's a good thing to keep in mind when you make ramen at home.

This chapter also contains a few simpler, shorter, self-contained ramen recipes like sōki soba (pages 184–185) and reimen (pages 190–191), which I'd recommend as good options if you're impatient to get into a bowl of noodles as soon as possible.

Broth

First of all: the broth. Broth is the soul of ramen. It is arguably the most important element in the bowl. It should be really packed with flavor, full of body, and, most importantly, it should be unique and reflect the taste and personality of the cook who makes it. The following recipes are for three base broths—pork, chicken and seafood—that can be used on their own or blended together.

Tonkotsu Broth
豚骨スープ

(Pork Bone Broth)

Tonkotsu ramen is one of the best-known dishes in Kyushu cuisine; it is practically synonymous with Fukuoka in particular. But there is no one standard for tonkotsu; there are innumerable variations from ramen shop to ramen shop, often in accordance with local styles, but just as often flamboyantly individualistic. Tonkotsu broth should always be deliciously creamy, cloudy (opaque, really) and whitish beige in color. Beyond that, you can decide how you like it and make it your own. You can go for the intensely porky tonkotsu of Kurume (pages 174–175), which is only coarsely sieved and has sandy bits of bone left in it, or you can cut it with chicken stock and soy sauce for the lighter but still very flavorful broth favored in Miyazaki (pages 182–183).

Yield:
about 10½ cups (2.5L)

Ingredients:
2 pig's feet (trotters), chopped or sawn in half
4½ lb (2kg) pork thigh bones, sawn in half
4¼ qt (4L) water, plus more for parboiling
½ onion
generous 1 oz (about 30g) mushrooms
½ bulb (1 oz [25g]) garlic
1 oz (25g) fresh ginger
¼ bulb fennel

Use a blowtorch or shave the pig's feet and rinse them under running water to remove hair and dirt. Cover the bones and pig's feet with water in a large stockpot and bring to the boil. Discard the water and rinse the bones; this is to leach blood from the bones, which would otherwise coagulate in the broth and make it scummy. Return to the pot, add 4¼ qt (4L) water and boil hard for at least 8 hours for a lighter broth, and up to 20 hours for a very dense, creamy, rich broth (the longest I've heard of tonkotsu broth being boiled is 60 hours). Skim any scum off the surface and top up with fresh water as needed. Add the vegetables and boil for another 2 hours. During this time, let the broth reduce slightly and taste it from time to time.

When the broth has reached the consistency and flavor you want, remove the bones, then strain the broth through a coarse sieve. You may notice that quite a lot of fat accumulates in the broth; don't skim this off! That fat works in conjunction with all the dissolved collagen from the bones to create the classic Kyushu ramen mouthfeel, which many describe as milky, creamy or gravy-like. It should be unctuous.

Torigara Broth

鶏ガラスープ

(Chicken Bone Broth)

This is my base chicken broth recipe, which I use in various ramen such as Nagasaki chanpon (pages 178–179) and Miyazaki ramen (pages 182–183). It's rich, deep and a little bit sweet, with an enticing and complex fragrance from the aromatics added. But add whatever you like to make it your own—fresh ginger, dried chilies, fennel, and so on. The main thing to remember is that it should never be bland or boring.

Yield:
about 1 qt (1 L)

Ingredients:
2 lb (900g) chicken bones, skin and trimmings
1 onion, roughly chopped
1 large carrot, roughly chopped
1 oz (30g) mushrooms, roughly chopped
½ bulb garlic
1 medium stick celery, roughly chopped
2 bay leaves
2 star anise
2 qt (2L) water
white pepper, to taste
garlic powder, to taste
ground ginger, to taste

If your chicken bones are raw, first draw out the blood. Put them in a stockpot with lightly salted water to cover. Bring to the boil, then discard the water and rinse the bones. (If you're using bones from a cooked chicken, skip this step.) Return the bones to the pot along with all the other ingredients, cover with a snug-fitting lid and boil hard for 6 hours, skimming off any scum (there should be very little due to the parboiling step) and adding more water as necessary. In the last hour or so of cooking, allow the stock to reduce. Pass the stock through a sieve, using the back of a ladle to squeeze out all the juice from the bones and vegetables. This should yield about 1 qt (1L) of broth—if you have much more or less than this, not to worry. Simply add or reduce until you're in the ballpark.

We are not looking for a clear, French-style stock here. The water should be at a rolling boil the whole time, and the resulting liquid will be very cloudy. There should be plenty of chicken fat that rises to the top of the broth once it's settled. As with the tonkotsu broth, don't skim the fat off. It's full of flavor and will give your soup a fantastic mouthfeel.

Gyokai Broth

魚介ズープ

(Seafood Broth)

Gyokai (seafood) broth isn't found in most Kyushu ramen, but I use it in Nagasaki chanpon (pages 178–179), where it complements the stir-fried shellfish topping. Like the tonkotsu and torigara broths, this has a pretty strong flavor (remember, the last thing ramen broth should be is bland), but it's a lot less heavy owing to less collagen and a much shorter, gentler boil.

This recipe calls for *niboshi,* which are little dried anchovy-type things. They're a little expensive and hard to come by, but there's a Southeast Asian alternative that I think works just as well—they're called *ikan bilis* and can be found in Asian markets usually labeled "dried fish" or "dried anchovy." In a way I actually prefer them to real niboshi, because niboshi have bitter heads and guts that have to be tediously removed. Ikan bilis have no such bitterness, but they are really salty, so they have to be soaked in a few changes of water before using.

Yield:
about 1 qt (1L)

Ingredients:
about 1½ oz (40g) niboshi or ikan bilis
3½ oz (100g) shrimp, crab or lobster shells
3½ oz (100g) white fish bones
1¾ oz (50g) dried shrimp or dried crayfish
1 bay leaf
1 onion, roughly chopped
¼ bulb fennel, roughly chopped
2 cloves garlic, roughly chopped
½ oz (15g) ginger, roughly chopped
5 cups (1.2L) water
6½ tbsp (100ml) sake
½–¾ oz (15–20g) kombu

Preheat the oven to 400°F. If you're using niboshi, remove the heads and guts. If you're using ikan bilis, soak them in three changes of water for 15 minutes each time and drain well. Smash up the shrimp, crab or lobster shells between two tea towels with a rolling pin or other blunt instrument. Place them on a baking sheet with the fish bones, dried shrimp and niboshi or ikan bilis, and bake for 20–30 minutes, until slightly colored and richly aromatic. Transfer everything to a large stockpot and add the bay leaf, onion, fennel, garlic and ginger. Add the water and sake, bring to the boil and simmer gently for 4 hours, skimming any scum off the surface.

Pass the broth through a sieve and, while still hot, add the kombu. Leave to infuse until cool, then pass through a fine sieve.

How to Season Your Ramen Broth

You can spend many devoted hours making a soulful, rich broth for your ramen, but if it isn't seasoned properly, then all that time and effort will be for nothing. David Chang has said that ramen broth should be very salty, on the brink of too salty. I agree, but it isn't just about salt—it's about umami, the fifth basic taste often translated as savoriness or meatiness.

The umami sensation is present in all food cultures and comes in many forms, most potently in the compounds inosinate, guanylate and glutamate. Inosinate is most frequently derived from fermented or cured meat and fish products, like ham, *nam pla* (fish sauce) or katsuobushi. Guanylate is found in high amounts in vegetables, especially dried mushrooms. And glutamate comes from all manner of vegetable and dairy products, often dried or fermented; kombu, Parmesan cheese, saukerkraut and Marmite have some of the highest concentrations. The most flavorful, umami-rich stocks call for a combination of all these elements. That's why my Nanban dashi uses shiitake in addition to the usual katsuobushi and kombu.

However, most ramen broths, being made from ingredients that aren't particularly rich in umami compounds, like uncured meat and fresh vegetables, need a bit of a boost. Salt is a good start, but there are other ingredients to use that can really take your broth from pretty good to slurp-down-every-last-drop good.

Salt

Salt, by itself, is the most pure way to season your ramen broth and is always necessary to add lusciousness—think of the can't-stop-eating-them quality of potato chips. Salt makes our taste buds stand to attention. It brings forward sweetness and heightens other flavors. It makes our mouths water.

Use good-quality sea salt, especially if you're using salt alone, because sea salt has more flavor compounds in it that bring sweetness, umami and character. And remember: too little salt is an easily remedied problem, but too much is an irrevocable disaster. Always start with a little, taste and then add more as needed. Your broth should be used to indirectly salt everything else in your ramen—the noodles and most of the toppings will rely on it for their seasoning, so use a little more than you might think is needed when tasting the broth on its own.

MSG

Using monosodium glutamate (MSG) is another very pure way to season ramen, introducing no extraneous flavors while adding lip-smacking, mouth-filling umami. Now, I know MSG gets a lot of bad press. This is completely unfounded. What began as a bogus, pseudoscientific affliction known as "Chinese restaurant syndrome" has been overblown into a persistent but utterly fictional worldwide epidemic. Countless studies have shown no negative health effects of MSG, except for a few that have reported neural damage in rats—but the rats were being fed around 1% of their body weight in MSG daily! That may not sound like much, but in human terms that would equate to over 1½ pounds (672g). That's insane.

I spoke to Peter Barham, a food scientist at the UK's University of Bristol, about MSG. He agreed that there is no rationale for any such nonsense as "Chinese restaurant syndrome," and described an informal experiment you can conduct on anyone who claims negative reactions to MSG. Feed your subject a homemade Chinese meal, and later, an Italian meal. Chances are he or she will have a reaction to the Chinese food, but not the Italian, even though they contain similar amounts of natural MSG. What this suggests is that certain people may have a psychosomatic reaction to MSG, or they are actually reacting to something found in conjunction with the MSG in Chinese food—soy, for example. But MSG itself isn't the culprit. Barham also noted that MSG may even be good for you, because it's a lower-sodium seasoning than salt, and it contains an essential amino acid.

If you're still not convinced about MSG, bear this in mind: you're already consuming it indirectly anyway. It's in soy sauce, it's in miso, it's in cheese, bacon, scallops and ketchup. It's everywhere. And you can use any of these things to umami-up your broth—the London ramen shop Ittenbari puts Marmite and tomatoes in its miso broth, while the now-defunct Mitsukoshi ramen used scallop extract. Momofuku's innovation was bacon dashi. But these ingredients carry extraneous flavors; by using pure MSG, you add that savory, satisfying character without anything getting in the way of the pure pork/chicken/seafood essence you worked so hard to achieve.

Just like anything else, MSG should never be used in excess. Start with a little, and try it in conjunction with salt—the two work in synergy. MSG is available at any Asian market, often under the brand Ajinomoto ("essence of flavor"). Buy a bag and experiment.

Dashi powder or stock powder

Dashi powder is a lovely way to finish good broth, bringing umami as well as a touch of sweetness and a delicately smoky, seaside flavor. However, I wouldn't use it by itself, as you'd have to use a lot of it to make the broth salty enough, and this can result in your broth tasting more like dashi than the bones you made it from. It's also somewhat expensive. I'd recommend using a little dashi powder and finishing the seasoning with plain salt. Another good option is to use a touch of Chinese chicken-stock powder. This may sound like a cheat, but just a pinch can add a nice, sweet umami that marries with the natural flavor of your stock rather than obscuring it.

Tare

Many ramen shops in Japan use a unique liquid seasoning base called tare—a term that can also describe a glaze or dipping sauce (see pages 24–25)—to flavor their broth. This is usually some sort of broth in and of itself, with a dashi, chicken or seafood base, flavored with soy sauce, mirin, sake and/or other elements to bring depth and harmony to the soup. However, I find it extraneous in most Kyushu ramen preparations, which are meant to taste of pork and pretty much only pork—strong dashi and soy sauce flavors in particular are a much more northern thing. But feel free to experiment! You can use the all-purpose tare recipe on pages 24–25 as a starting point, but omit the cornstarch and sugar, use less soy sauce and add a bit of kombu dashi.

Soy sauce

Certain ramen recipes, like that from Miyazaki, call for soy sauce as the primary seasoning. I quite like a good shōyu ramen, which has a nice, rich umami and a slight acidity, but it's out of place in other versions. Hakata ramen and Kurume ramen, for example,

should taste almost purely of pig and be very light in color; soy sauce will obviously be counterproductive to those ends. As a general rule, I use just a little soy sauce in conjunction with other seasonings, so that it doesn't completely overwhelm the broth.

Miso

Miso is unusual in southern Japanese ramen and favored more in northern prefectures. That said, it is delicious, so if authenticity is not a priority, stir some into your stock. Because it's a thick paste rather than a sauce or powder, it has the added bonus of amplifying the body of your broth. My favorite miso ramen are almost chowder-like in their creaminess.

Kombu and katsuobushi

For a subtle, more refined umami character, you can treat your finished broth like the base for a light dashi. Simply let kombu and katsuobushi infuse into the broth exactly as you would for a dashi (see pages 38–39). This results in a lovely (if expensive) broth, but it will need a boost from salt—there isn't enough occurring naturally in the seaweed and fish for them to act as stand-alone seasonings.

White pepper and garlic powder

White pepper doesn't add umami to broth, but to me, it's indispensable. There's something about the muskiness of it that really heightens the flavor of pork in particular, while its light spice helps balance out tonkotsu's richness. Don't go crazy with it—too much pepper is pretty unpleasant. But I use at least a pinch in every broth I make. Likewise, I find that a restrained pinch of garlic powder adds character to broth (especially chicken).

Your own blend: Mix and match

I use a blend of seasonings in my broths, not only to give them a complete, rounded flavor but also to achieve better consistency between batches. I am not going to tell you exactly what quantities go into it, but here's the gist of it: sea salt, dashi powder, white pepper, garlic powder, dried ginger and kombu. Sorry, I won't divulge the full recipe; that's something I will take to my grave. But anyway, it's not about my ramen—it's about your ramen, and this is just to give you an idea of how best to achieve the broth that most satisfies your specific palate.

Alkaline Noodles
ラーメン

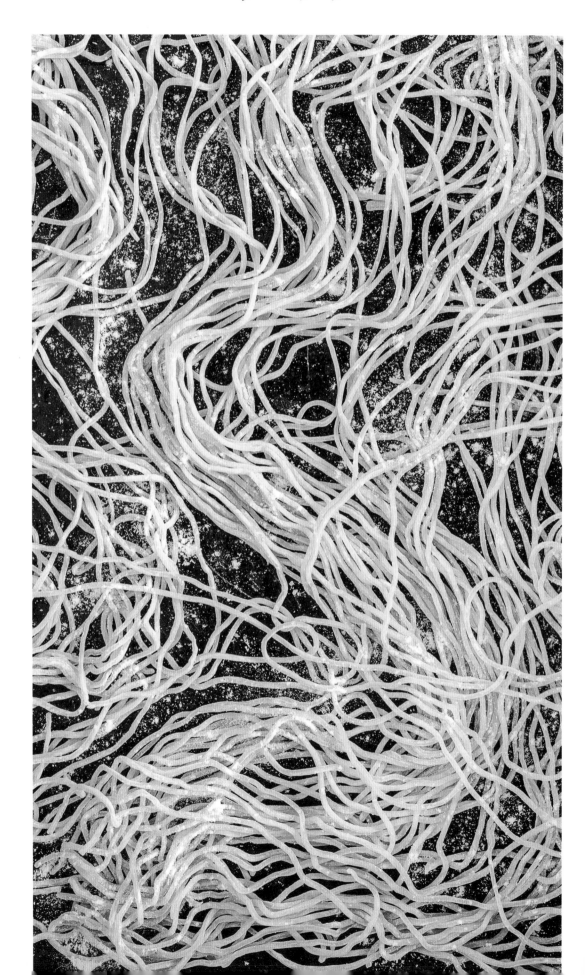

One key feature that separates ramen from other, similar noodle soups is the noodles themselves. They are made with alkaline salts—potassium carbonate and sodium carbonate—which disrupt gluten formation in the noodles and give them their characteristic springy texture and yellowish color. In Japan these salts, or more accurately a solution of them in water, are called *kansui*, which simply means "lye water" or "salt water," depending on how it's written. Apparently the origins of making noodles with these compounds can be found in communities around the salt lakes of Mongolia, where the water is naturally full of alkaline minerals. You can order potassium carbonate or sodium carbonate from online chemical suppliers (very strange what you can get on the Internet these days), but if you can't get them, you can make your own. Simply cook baking soda on a foil-lined baking sheet in the oven at 250°F for about an hour. The heat breaks down the double carbon bond into carbonate of soda, a.k.a. sodium carbonate. Handle it carefully; because of its strong alkalinity, it can irritate the skin.

If all of this sounds a bit too much, don't worry: you don't have to make your own noodles to make good ramen. Most ramen shops don't, as this requires time, space and expensive equipment. Instead, they get them from big noodle manufacturers, often made to individualized parameters using bespoke recipes. Asian markets in the UK and US supply a good range of fresh alkaline noodles—look out for noodles from a company called Sun Brand.

However, making your own noodles has some advantages. First of all, you can cut them to any thickness you prefer. Also, they will come out paler in color (which is somewhat more authentically Kyushu) as most of the factory-made ones use beta-carotene as a coloring. Plus, you can add another dimension of flavor to your ramen in the noodles themselves—in my recipe, I use a little white pepper and sesame oil to this end. In Japan I've had noodles flavored with garlic and chili, as well.

So do give this a go if you're so inclined. Your ramen may be a little better if you make your own noodles, but it won't be much worse if you don't.

Yield:

8 servings

Ingredients:

about 6⅓ cups (800g) type 00 flour (pasta flour), plus more for dusting
5 eggs
¼ oz (6g) sodium carbonate and/or potassium carbonate
7 tbsp (110ml) water
2 tbsp (30ml) sesame oil
pinch white pepper
½ tsp fine salt

Combine all the ingredients in a stand mixer with a dough hook. Mix for 10 minutes, until a coarse, dry dough is formed; if the dough is too crumbly, add a tiny bit more water. If it's too wet, add a little more flour. Knead until smooth; it should feel like the soft skin of your lover's cheek (or something). Wrap the dough in plastic wrap and refrigerate for at least 30 minutes. Cut off a workable portion of dough and roll out into a rectangle on a floured work surface. Roll through a pasta machine, flouring as needed, until it is rolled out to the 2mm setting.

For recipes calling for thin noodles, keep rolling out to the 1.5mm setting. Cut the noodles using the 1.5mm cutter attachment (for capellini). For recipes calling for thick noodles, keep the dough at 2mm and cut using the spaghetti attachment.

Divide the cut noodles into 8 portions and dredge them in a little flour to keep them from sticking, shaking off the excess. Keep each portion wrapped in plastic wrap and refrigerated until ready to use. Noodles should be made on the same day you plan to cook them.

Ramen Toppings

The following recipes are for common ramen toppings. They add texture, character and balance to ramen, so don't neglect them. Many of these should be put into the bowl directly before serving (as per the full ramen recipes), but some can be served on the side, to be used as needed.

Tea-pickled Eggs
紅茶漬けのゆで卵

One of the most common toppings is *ajitama*, a marinated boiled egg. In Japan, tea is not typically used in recipes for marinated eggs, but I think it works beautifully. The idea comes from Hong Kong, where lovely boiled eggs that have been marbled by a soak in black tea are sold as street snacks. I use Lapsang souchong to give the eggs a subtle smokiness.

They aren't just good for ramen, by the way—they make a fantastic salty snack by themselves, or, smashed up with some mayo, English mustard and scallions, a great sandwich filling.

Yield:
6 eggs

Ingredients:
For the pickling liquid:
1¼ cups (300ml) dashi (pages 38–39)
    or vegetarian dashi (pages 40–41)
1 star anise
2 Lapsang souchong tea bags
7 tbsp (110ml) soy sauce
3¼ tbsp (50ml) mirin
3¼ tbsp (50ml) rice vinegar

For the eggs:
6 eggs—get the best-quality eggs you can
lots of ice

For the pickling liquid:
Bring the dashi and the star anise to the boil. Remove from heat and add the Lapsang souchong; leave to infuse for 20 minutes. Strain and add the soy sauce, mirin and rice vinegar. Set aside.

For the eggs:
Boiling eggs is a surprisingly tricky business. If you have a method that works for you, by all means, use that. But this method always gives me perfect results: the yolks are set just along their outsides and still nice and gooey in the middle. If you are not confident in your egg-boiling and peeling skills, do a test run with a couple of extra eggs before cooking the rest. That way, you should end up with 6 perfect eggs.

First prepare an ice bath: fill a large bowl or container with ice and cover with cold water. Fill a saucepan, large enough to contain a metal sieve, colander or steamer basket, with water and bring to a rapid boil. Boil the eggs in batches: place a few eggs in your colander or sieve and lower it into the boiling water. Make sure all the eggs are totally covered and that the water temperature doesn't drop too much when you put them in the pot. Boil the eggs for exactly 6 minutes and 20 seconds, then lift them out and transfer them to the ice bath to stop the cooking. Repeat for the rest of the eggs.

Peel the eggs under water and place them in the pickling liquid. Marinate in the refrigerator for 24–48 hours before using.

Chāshū

チャーシュー

(Cola-braised Pork Belly)

The toppings in a bowl of ramen are like an ensemble cast. They all play off each other in a delightful theater of contrasting textures and flavors. But for many, the chāshū is the star of the show. Derived from the Cantonese *char siu*, the roast pork most famously known as the filling of *char siu bao*, it is a ramen staple—I always feel that a bowl is incomplete without it. The pork is braised to a pillowy soft texture that almost acts as a solid iteration of the liquid broth. Indeed, many ramen shops braise their chāshū in their broth. Not me, however. I use cola. The idea comes from both Chinese and American pork recipes, and while it may sound strange, think about all the flavors you get from cola: dark sugar, vanilla, citrus, anise, clove, cinnamon—all things that complement pork perfectly.

Yield:
enough for 4–6 bowls of ramen,
or 2 servings as a main

Ingredients:
1⅓ cups (330ml) cola
6½ tbsp (100ml) soy sauce
2 tbsp (30ml) rice vinegar
14 oz (400g) pork belly, rind removed

Preheat the oven to 250°F.

Combine the liquid ingredients and pour over the pork belly in a casserole dish. Cover with a lid or foil and braise in the oven until very tender, about 4 hours. Since oven temperatures vary, after 2 hours check the belly for tenderness with a fork, and then every half hour. Dried-out, tough chāshū is rather sad. When the pork is almost falling apart, remove it from the oven. Leave to cool. Place a plate or second baking dish on top of the belly pork to press it down, then transfer to the fridge and chill in its braising liquid until completely cool.

Remove the pork from its cooking liquid. Separate out the fat, which can be used like lard for cooking, and the reduced braising liquid, which should have turned to a soft jelly—this can be used in marinades or for your all-purpose tare (pages 24–25).

Slice the pork belly thinly across the grain, no more than ³⁄₁₆ inch (5mm) thick so that it can be easily handled with chopsticks. The sliced chāshū can be reheated in a hot oven or dry frying pan, or by dipping it briefly in simmering broth.

Namool

ナムル

(Spicy Bean Sprouts)

This is originally a Korean *banchan*, one of myriad little side dishes served in a typical Korean meal. Once at a restaurant in Busan, Laura and I ordered five dishes, but when we counted the plates on the table, there were a total of 22 thanks to all the banchan. *Namool* really just means "seasoned vegetables," but in Japan, it almost invariably refers to *sukju namool*, made from bean sprouts. Traditionally seasoned with just salt and sesame oil, in their transposition across the Korea Strait, they became spicy—which is odd, since most Korean foods get their spice toned down when they make the move to Japan. Namool has been heartily welcomed into ramen shops around Fukuoka, where it is often found in little jars on the table alongside soy sauce, minced garlic and other toppings. They're more addictive than bean sprouts have any right to be, and are a great side dish for all kinds of meaty meals.

Yield:
enough for 8–10 bowls of ramen,
or 2–4 side dishes

Ingredients:
½ tsp salt
10½ oz (300g) bean sprouts
1 tbsp sesame oil
1 clove garlic, chopped
1 scallion, finely sliced
1 tbsp *tobanjian* (Chinese chili bean paste) or gochujang (Korean fermented chili paste)
1 tsp sesame seeds
1 tsp rice vinegar

Sprinkle the salt over the bean sprouts in a bowl and let them sit for 15 minutes or so to draw out some of the liquid. Rinse them under cold water and squeeze them dry.

Place the sesame oil in a frying pan over medium heat, then lightly sauté the garlic and scallion, and stir the tobanjian or gochujang into the oil. Add the bean sprouts and toss them through the sauce, cooking for just 1–2 minutes. Add the sesame seeds and vinegar and remove from the heat.

You can eat these right away, but I find they taste better after at least one night in the fridge, and they will keep for up to a week.

Takana-zuke

高菜漬け

(Spicy Pickled Mustard Greens)

In Japan, *takana-zuke* is an inexpensive pickle often offered for free at ramen shops, sitting on the counter alongside other typical condiments like garlic or chili oil. However, buying pickled takana in the UK, considering it's just greens, chili and salt, is exceedingly pricy. You're better off making your own—it's easy and much tastier. Mustard greens are sold at specialty grocers or at most Asian markets, where they are called *kai choi*, and they have a pleasant horseradish-like bite that is accentuated by chili and the fermentation process. I have noticed that much of the mustard greens in the UK are less "mustardy" than in Japan, so, if necessary, I add a little bit of hot mustard to punch up the taste.

Yield:
about 1⅛ lb (500g)

Ingredients:
1⅛–1⅝ lb (500–700g) mustard greens
1 tbsp salt
1 tbsp (3g) hot chili powder, or more to taste
1–3 tsp hot mustard (optional)

Cut or tear the mustard leaves from their tough bottom stems. Lay the leaves flat in a container, sprinkling the salt and chili powder between each layer. When you've laid all the leaves down, give them a good bash with your fist; you want to break up the greens' cells and let the salt penetrate to extract their natural juices that will become a brine.

When the leaves are damp to the touch, squeeze them and bash them some more, being careful not to tear them too much (although that's really just for aesthetic reasons). Weight the leaves down with a heavy object that fits the container snugly—this could be a bottle of booze, another container filled with something heavy or a sealed plastic bag filled with water—whatever works. Make sure that enough juice has come out of the greens to submerge them, then cover loosely with a cloth or plastic wrap, securing with a string or rubber band.

Leave to sit at room temperature for 4 days (less if it's warm in your kitchen, more if it's cold). Have a look and a taste. When it's noticeably sour, it's ready—remove the weight and transfer the pickle to the fridge, where it will keep for weeks. At this point, you can work in more chili powder and/or some mustard if you want it spicier. Chop into small pieces before serving.

Flavor Bombs

味爆弹

The following "flavor bombs" are made to change the flavor of ramen as you eat it; they're solid when the bowl is served but gradually melt to make the broth richer, sweeter and spicier the farther down you go. They aren't just for ramen, though—add them to stir-fries, stews or all manner of soups to impart a fantastic whack of flavor wherever it is needed.

Yuzu-koshō Pork Fat

柚子胡椒豚脂

If you make chāshū (pages 162–163) or any of the other pork belly recipes in this book, chances are you'll end up with some very useful by-products. The first is a soft jelly comprising pork juice and reduced braising liquid; put this in your all-purpose tare (pages 24–25) or use it to season ramen. The second is a flavorful layer of white fat. I'm sure you can find many uses for this—it even makes a good substitute for butter in sweets. But I think it's fantastic melted right back into ramen, especially seasoned with yuzu-koshō. It has the effect of adding richness to the broth and simultaneously contrasting it with spicy citrus. A good choice for fans of really intense flavors.

Yield:
about 7–8 bombs

Ingredients:
3½–4½ oz (100–125g) rendered pork fat
(or lard), at room temperature
1 oz (25g) yuzu-koshō

Mash the ingredients together, using a fork or spoon, until evenly combined. Chill in the fridge, then portion into small balls using a melon baller or by rolling it between your palms.

Shiitake Seaweed Butter

椎茸海藻バター

Unlike the other bombs, which add spice, these add concentrated umami. They are deep and meaty, with a remarkable mushroom aroma and a faintly sweet aftertaste. This recipe makes more than you'll need for a few bowls of ramen, but they're great in all kinds of dishes—melt them into miso soup or rub them onto steaks before cooking.

Yield:
about 6 bombs

Ingredients:
⅓ oz (10g) dried shiitake
7 tbsp (100g) butter
2 tbsp aonoriko (green seaweed flakes)
pinch salt

Process the shiitake in a food processor or blender for a few minutes—try to get them down to a very fine powder. Melt the butter in a saucepan, add the powdered shiitake and cook over a gentle heat for about 10 minutes; the mushroom powder should absorb the butter and the mixture should become pasty. Stir in the aonoriko and salt and refrigerate until firmly set. Portion into balls using a melon baller or by rolling pieces between your palms.

Spicy Miso Butter
辛みそバター

Spicy miso butter provides what I think of as a "complete" flavor: salty, sweet, spicy, tangy, umami and fatty all in one. It's so good I often find myself wanting to put it in everything I make—it's particularly good with grilled mushrooms (pages 140–141).

Yield:
about 7–8 bombs

Ingredients:
3 tbsp (25g) chili powder (preferably Korean)
3½ tbsp (50g) butter, at room temperature
4½ tbsp (75g) red miso

Mash everything together, using a whisk or fork, until evenly combined. Chill in the fridge, then portion into balls either by using a melon baller or by rolling pieces between your palms.

Complete Ramen Recipes

The preceding recipes have shown you the elements of ramen. Feel free to combine them in any way you like. The following recipes use these elements, and a few new ones, to show you how to make both traditional and modern ramen dishes.

Hakata-style Ramen

博多ラーメン

(Pork Broth Ramen)

"Hakata ramen" is the first thing that comes up in Google autocomplete when you search for Hakata, a bustling district in central Fukuoka. Hakata ramen's rich stock and thin noodles have charmed all of Japan and now much of the world, fueling an ongoing ramen boom.

This is a fairly orthodox recipe for Hakata ramen; the only thing unusual about it is that I use green māyu rather than the traditional black, which you should choose instead if you want the fully authentic Hakata ramen experience. Either way, it is an extraordinarily involving bowl of food.

Yield:
2 servings

Ingredients:
2 portions thin noodles
3–3⅓ cups (700–800ml) tonkotsu broth
    (seasoned), at a simmer (pages 150–151)
1½ oz (40g) cabbage, julienned and
    blanched in the broth
4 slices chāshū, reheated (pages 162–163)
2 tsp green or black māyu (pages 30–31)
2 tea-pickled eggs, sliced in half
    (pages 160–161)
¾ oz (20g) beni shōga
1 scallion, finely sliced
toasted sesame seeds

Cook the noodles in rapidly boiling water until al dente: they should have a good bite to them. Transfer to a bowl and pour the broth over them, then top with the blanched cabbage, chāshū, māyu, eggs, beni shōga, scallion and sesame seeds, in that order. Slurp while piping hot.

Kurume-style Ramen
久留米ラーメン

(Rich and Rustic Pork Broth Ramen)

Kurume is a city in the south of Fukuoka prefecture, and some people—mostly Kurume residents—say it is the original, ancestral home of tonkotsu ramen. In reality, tonkotsu was probably created in Nagasaki by Chinese immigrants, but never mind that. Kurume ramen certainly tastes like something from another era; many Kurume shops usually describe their richest ramen as *mukashii*, meaning "from back in the day." It's even thicker than its Hakata cousin and famous for being only roughly sieved, which means bowls usually have chalky bits of bone in them. It is pure, obliterated pig.

This is "advanced level" ramen because the broth takes a lot of time to make, and the end product is really, really intense and rustic. I'd recommend trying the Hakata ramen first, and if it just isn't porky enough for you, set aside a weekend to try this.

Yield:
2 servings

Ingredients:
3–3⅓ cups (700–800ml) Kurume ramen stock (see method below)
6½–8 tbsp (100–120ml) soy sauce
¾ oz (20g) dried black fungus
2 portions thin or medium noodles
⅓–½ oz (10–15g) rendered pork fat—I'd recommend using the stuff that comes off your chāshū
4 slices chāshū, reheated (pages 162–163)
2 medium-boiled eggs, cut in half
2 scallions, finely sliced
¾ oz (20g) beni shōga, or more to taste
1 sheet nori, cut into 6 rectangles
toasted sesame seeds

To make the stock, follow the instructions for tonkotsu broth (pages 150–151), but add half a pig skull (yes, really—ask your butcher) and an extra pig's foot. Boil for at least 12 hours, but I'd recommend 16–20 hours. Alternatively, if you have some tonkotsu broth ready, you can just add the half skull and extra pig's foot to that and boil it up for another 8 hours or so. Pass your finished stock through a coarse sieve; it should have lots of bits left in it. Season with white pepper and sea salt, MSG and/or kombu—keep the pork flavor pure.

Pour the soy sauce over the black fungus and leave to sit for 20–30 minutes to rehydrate. Reheat the broth if necessary. Cook the noodles in rapidly boiling water until al dente—but only just. Transfer to a bowl and pour the broth over them, then top with the pork fat, chāshū, eggs, scallions, beni shōga, nori and sesame seeds, in that order. Slurp while piping hot. You may want to serve this with a little vinegar, yuzu-koshō or even mentaiko (pages 50–51) on the side—a little acidity or spice helps take the edge off if it's too rich.

Kumamoto-style Ramen

熊本ラーメン

(Pork Broth Ramen with Fried Garlic)

This is my favorite ramen. It's almost identical to Hakata ramen, but with one important addition: fried garlic chips. They give the bowl a wonderfully stinky odor that perfumes and enhances the porky broth, without the harshness of raw garlic. Lovely, lovely stuff. Just don't expect a make-out session after dinner unless you've got some powerful chewing gum.

Yield:
2 servings

Ingredients:
1 tbsp vegetable oil
4 cloves garlic, thinly sliced
pinch salt
2 portions thin noodles
3–3⅓ cups (700–800ml) seasoned tonkotsu
    broth (pages 150–151), at a simmer
about 1½ oz (40g) cabbage, julienned and
    blanched in the broth
4 slices chāshū (pages 162–163), reheated
2 tbsp black māyu (page 31)
2 tea-pickled eggs (pages 160–161), sliced
    in half, or onsen eggs (pages 54–55)
¾ oz (20g) beni shōga
1 scallion, finely sliced
toasted sesame seeds

Heat the vegetable oil in a small pan over a medium heat. Fry the garlic until golden, about 2–3 minutes, stirring often. Be very careful not to let the garlic burn, or it will be bitter and sad. Drain on paper towels and season with salt.

Cook the noodles in rapidly boiling water until al dente, then transfer to a bowl. Pour the broth over them, then top with the cabbage, chāshū, māyu, eggs, beni shōga, scallion, garlic chips and sesame seeds, in that order.

Nagasaki-style Chanpon
長崎ちゃんぽん

(Blend of Seafood, Chicken and Pork Broth with Stir-fried Seafood)

Nagasaki is where most Chinese immigrants in Japan settled before the 20th century, and it is where much of ramen's origins lie. Chanpon was a sort of proto-ramen, a hearty noodle soup invented by Nagasaki expat chef Chen Pingjun, using pork bones and a stir-fry of inexpensive miscellaneous scraps of vegetables and off-cuts of pork. Today it is something more extravagant (but still decidedly casual), topped with a melange of colorful shellfish and fresh vegetables. This recipe calls for *kamaboko, naruto* or *chikuwa*—these are bouncy-textured fish cakes that can be found in the freezer sections of Asian grocery stores.

Yield:

2 servings

Ingredients:

1½–1⅔ cups (350–400ml) tonkotsu broth
 (pages 150–151) or torigara broth
 (pages 152–153), or a mix of both
1½–1⅔ cups (350–400ml) gyokai broth
 (pages 154–155) or dashi (pages 38–41)
sea salt
white pepper
1 clove garlic, chopped
1¾ oz (50g) bean sprouts
1¾ oz (50g) cabbage, sliced into ⅜-inch
 (1cm) pieces
¾ oz (20g) beni shōga
8–10 large raw shrimp
1 squid, cut into ⅜-inch (1cm) rings
3½ oz (100g) scallops
vegetable oil, for stir-frying
1¾ oz (50g) kamaboko, naruto or chikuwa
 (fish cakes), sliced (optional)
2 scallions, sliced
2 portions thick noodles
sesame oil, to drizzle
toasted sesame seeds, to sprinkle

Combine the broths, bring to a simmer and then season well. Stir-fry the garlic, bean sprouts, cabbage, beni shōga, shrimp, squid and scallops in vegetable oil over a very high heat until everything is cooked through—about 4–5 minutes. Add the kamaboko (if using) and scallions to warm through. Season with sea salt and white pepper.

Cook the noodles until al dente. Transfer to a bowl and pour on the broth. Top with the stir-fry and finish with a light drizzle of sesame oil and a sprinkle of sesame seeds.

Kagoshima-style Ramen

鹿児島ラーメン

(Lighter Pork Broth Ramen with Extra Pork)

Kagoshima, the southernmost prefecture in mainland Japan, is famous for its delicious pork. And yet, it's not the porkiest ramen in Kyushu—that distinction must go to Kurume ramen (pages 174–175). In fact, Kagoshima ramen tends to be among the lightest of the tonkotsu type, blended with dashi for a more "Japanese" flavor. Of course, there are exceptions to this—some Kagoshima ramen shops make the most of the very fatty pork available to them to produce ramen that is devastatingly smooth and unctuous. It's up to you which Kagoshima ramen route to go down—here's the path I chose. The broth is a little lighter, but everybody gets a double portion of chāshū. Win-win!

Yield:

2 servings

Ingredients:

2½–3 cups (600–700ml) Kagoshima tonkotsu broth (see method below), or use half tonkotsu broth and half chicken broth

6½–8 tbsp (100–120ml) soy sauce

¾ oz (20g) dried black fungus

1 shallot, diced

2 tbsp vegetable oil

6½ tbsp (100ml) dashi

2 portions medium noodles

2 tbsp (30ml) black māyu (pages 30–31), optional

8 slices chāshū, reheated (pages 162–163)

2 tea-pickled eggs, sliced in half (pages 160–161)

¾ oz (20g) cabbage, cut into ⅜-inch (1cm) strips and blanched

1 scallion, finely sliced

¾ oz (20g) beni shōga, pickled daikon, takana-zuke, bamboo shoot or other Japanese pickles (or combine several)

toasted sesame seeds

To make the stock, follow the instructions for tonkotsu broth (pages 150–151), but double the quantities of vegetables and use only one pig's foot.

Pour the soy sauce over the black fungus and leave to sit for 20–30 minutes to rehydrate. Sauté the shallot in hot oil until golden brown. Combine the broth and dashi, reheat and season. Cook the noodles in rapidly boiling water just until al dente. Transfer the noodles to a bowl and pour on the broth, then top with the māyu (if using), chāshū, eggs, cabbage, shallot, scallion, pickles and sesame seeds, in that order. Slurp while piping hot.

Miyazaki-style Ramen

宮崎ラーメン

(Chicken, Pork and Soy Sauce Ramen)

Miyazaki is famous for chicken, which features in its ramen broth, but it is still within the locus of Fukuoka's tonkotsu hegemony. So Miyazaki ramen generally features a blend of chicken and pork broths, seasoned with soy sauce. If you don't want to go to the trouble of making two broths, you can use all chicken and it will still be delicious, or you can just chuck a pig's foot (prepared as on pages 150–151) in with your chicken broth as it boils.

Yield:
2 servings

Ingredients:
¾ oz (20g) dried black fungus
2–3¼ tbsp (30–50ml) soy sauce, to taste
splash of vinegar
1½–1⅔ cups (350–400ml) tonkotsu broth
  (pages 150–151)
1½–1⅔ cups (350–400ml) torigara broth
  (pages 152–153)
2 portions thin noodles
4 slices chāshū, reheated (pages 162–163)
1½–1¾ oz (40–50g) bean sprouts, stir-fried
2 tea-pickled eggs, sliced in half
  (pages 160–161)
¾ oz (20g) beni shōga
1 scallion, finely sliced
toasted sesame seeds

Rehydrate the fungus: put it in a bowl and cover with boiling water and a splash of soy sauce and vinegar and leave to steep for about 20 minutes—the fungus has absolutely no flavor without them. Discard any unabsorbed liquid before adding to the broth.

Combine the broths and the rest of the soy sauce and bring to a simmer. Cook the noodles in rapidly boiling water until al dente. Transfer to a bowl and pour on the broth, then top with the black fungus, chāshū, bean sprouts, eggs, beni shōga, scallion and sesame seeds, in that order.

Sōki Soba

ソーキそば

(Okinawan Pork Rib Ramen with a Light Dashi-pork Broth)

Despite this being a pork broth ramen, it has a much shorter boil and therefore a lighter flavor and consistency than Kyushu's standard tonkotsu ramen—in fact, it would probably be classed as a shōyu ramen because it is seasoned with a good glug of soy sauce. This is an iconic dish of Okinawa, famous for its love of pig. *Sōki* means "rib" in the local dialect, and *soba* is simply an antiquated term for noodles. Of all the ramen recipes in this book, this is probably the easiest, so if you have a craving and don't have 16 hours to spare for boiling bones, give it a go.

Yield:
2 servings

Ingredients:
For the broth and ribs:
½ rack pork loin ribs (about 6 ribs),
trimmed of cartilage
3⅓–3¾ cups (800–900ml) dashi
3¼ tbsp (50ml) soy sauce
1 tbsp awamori, shochu or sake
½ leek
1 clove garlic
1 star anise
⅓ oz (10g) fresh ginger
1 dried red chili

To serve:
reserved pork loin ribs
3½ oz (100g) bean sprouts
1 tbsp sesame oil
1 tsp white sesame seeds
salt and white pepper, to taste
reserved broth
2 portions medium-thick ramen noodles
2 tea-pickled eggs, sliced in half
(pages 160–161)
2 nira, finely sliced
6 slices takuan/pickled daikon
(about 1½ oz [40g])
Chili oil or chili vinegar, to taste

For the broth and ribs:
Cover the ribs in cold water and bring to the boil to leach out their blood. Discard the water and rinse the ribs, then place them in the dashi along with all the other broth ingredients and bring to the boil. Cover and reduce to a medium simmer, skimming any scum off the surface as necessary. Let them cook for about 2½ hours, until the ribs are quite soft—keep in mind you'll be eating this with chopsticks and a spoon, so they need to come off the bone fairly effortlessly. Remove and reserve the ribs and pass the broth through a fine sieve.

To serve:
Being careful not to tear the meat from the bone, separate the ribs with a sharp knife. Sauté the bean sprouts in the sesame oil with the sesame seeds, salt and pepper for just a few minutes so they retain some of their crunch. Reheat the broth and the ribs, if necessary. Cook the noodles in rapidly boiling water until a little softer than al dente. To assemble: pour the broth into bowls, slide in the noodles, then add the eggs, ribs (about 3 per person), bean sprouts, nira and takuan. Serve with chili oil or chili vinegar.

Grand Champion Ramen

マスターシェフラーメン

(Porcini and Tonkotsu Broth with Truffled Lobster Gyoza)

This is not authentic Kyushu ramen, that's for sure, but it is a winner, and I mean that quite literally. I cooked it in the *MasterChef* final as part of my winning menu. It's got rich tonkotsu broth as its base, with cheffy and luxurious flourishes like porcini, black truffle and lobster to send it over the top, almost into the realm of fine dining. Almost.

Yield:
2 servings

Ingredients:
For the broth:
⅓–½ oz (10–15g) kombu
⅓ oz (10g) dried porcini mushrooms, rinsed
1⅔ cups (400ml) water
¼ oz (.5g) katsuobushi
1⅔ cups (400ml) tonkotsu broth
(pages 150–151)
1 tsp soy sauce
1 tsp mirin
1 tsp sake
½ tsp rice vinegar
sea salt, to taste

For the gyoza:
meat from 1 smallish lobster tail (raw),
chopped
¼ oz (6–8g) fresh black truffle, grated
6–8 chives, finely sliced
pinch salt
pinch white pepper
6 gyoza wrappers

For the ramen:
porcini-tonkotsu broth
1–2 tbsp vegetable oil
reserved porcini
truffled lobster gyoza
2 portions thin or medium ramen noodles
few drops of good-quality truffle oil (optional)
4 slices chāshū (pages 162–163)
2 tsp black māyu (page 31)
2 tsp green māyu (page 31)
16 enoki mushrooms, trimmed to about
2 inches (5cm) in length
2 scallions, white parts only, finely julienned
2–2⅜ inches (5–6cm) rhubarb, finely
julienned

For the broth:
Place the kombu and mushrooms in the water and bring to a simmer. Remove from heat, add the katsuobushi and leave to infuse for at least 20 minutes. Reserve the porcini and discard the kombu and katsuobushi. Pass the soaking liquor (dashi) through a fine sieve or coffee filter, and blend together with the tonkotsu, soy sauce, mirin, sake and vinegar. Taste and add salt as needed. Pat the reserved mushrooms on paper towels until completely dry to the touch.

For the ramen:
Reheat your broth and keep it at a simmer. Heat the oil in a deep frying pan and sauté the reserved porcini until browned and crisp. Drain on paper towels. Cook the gyoza for 3–4 minutes on both sides. Boil the noodles until al dente, then drain and transfer to ramen bowls. Pour on the broth, then top with the porcini, truffle oil (if using), chāshū, māyu, gyoza, enoki, scallions and rhubarb.

For the gyoza:
Mix together all the filling ingredients and assemble the gyoza as per the instructions on pages 60–61.

Hunter Ramen

ハンターラーメン

A little while ago I bought a grouse and decided to make it into ramen. That may sound unorthodox, and it is, but I recently learned that before the mid-19th century, game was fair game in Japanese cooking. A friend said it reminded him of "hunter ramen," a specialty of a ramen shop called Tōka in Niigata prefecture. Apparently, it was made from mallard and was meanly ridiculed on a TV program seeking out Japan's worst ramen—a dubious distinction now featured on Tōka's own website. This is my tribute to Tōka's hunter ramen and to all the other ramen chefs who dare to be different—in my mind, that's what ramen is all about.

Yield:
2 servings

Ingredients:
For the broth:
1 grouse
3¾ cups (900ml) pork or chicken stock
1 star anise
2 bay leaves
⅓ oz (10g) fresh ginger, chopped
1 clove garlic, chopped
1 small onion (3½ oz [100g]), chopped
1 tbsp (15g) Hatchō miso
pinch white pepper, to taste
pinch sea salt, to taste

For the gyoza:
reserved grouse legs and wings
⅝ cup (150ml) sesame oil
7 tbsp (100g) butter or duck/goose fat
2 white nira, finely sliced
big pinch salt

Ingredients *continued*:
pinch white pepper
pinch sanshō or finely ground Szechuan pepper
6 gyoza wrappers

For the ramen:
½ tsp salt
1 tbsp mirin
2 tbsp rice vinegar
⅓–½ oz (10–15g) fresh ginger, cut into a fine julienne
reserved grouse breasts
butter, for frying
½ leek (white part), sliced on the bias about 1/16 inch (2mm) thick
4 shiitake mushrooms, stems removed and thinly sliced
2¾–3 cups (650–700ml) grouse broth
2 portions medium-thickness ramen noodles
2 onsen eggs (pages 54–55)
4 white nira, thinly sliced

For the broth:
Joint the grouse: remove the legs and wings and discard their skin, then remove the breasts and set aside. Place the carcass in a pan of cold water, bring to the boil and simmer for a minute to leach out the blood. Discard the water, rinse the carcass and add to a large stockpot with the stock, star anise, bay leaves, ginger, garlic and onion. Cover, bring to the boil and simmer on very low for 6 hours, until the stock is reduced by about a quarter, skimming any scum off the surface. Pass the broth through a fine sieve, then whisk in the miso, pepper and salt.

For the gyoza:
Preheat the oven to 225°F. Place the legs and wings in a small casserole dish, pour the sesame oil over and add the butter or fat. Put in the oven and cook the grouse for 4 hours, turning the meat halfway through cooking. Leave the confit to cool, then remove the meat, strain the fat through a fine sieve and reserve. Pick the meat off the bones, checking for tiny bones or cartilage. Chop the meat into a rough mince and mix in the nira, salt and peppers. Assemble the gyoza as per the instructions on pages 60–61.

For the ramen:
Preheat the oven to its lowest setting. Stir together the salt, mirin and vinegar until the salt is dissolved. Pour it over the ginger, and pickle for at least 2 hours. Season the grouse breasts with salt and fry in foaming butter for 3–4 minutes on each side, making sure they don't get too firm. Cover with foil and keep hot in the oven until ready to serve. Stir-fry the leek until brown in the confit fat, then remove and drain on paper towels. Stir-fry the mushrooms until soft and remove. Sauté the gyoza on both sides until golden brown, then add a splash of water to the pan and immediately cover so the gyoza steam through. Remove the grouse breasts from the oven and let them rest for about 5 minutes before slicing across the grain. Reheat the broth and cook the noodles in rapidly boiling water for 1 minute and drain. Pour the broth into bowls, then add the noodles, mushrooms, sliced grouse breast, eggs, gyoza, leek and nira, in that order. If you like, add a spoonful of the confit fat to each bowl for even more gamey richness.

Reimen

冷麵

(Korean-style Chilled Ramen)

Chilled noodle dishes in Japan usually feature udon, soba or somen, not ramen, but one exception is a Korean-influenced dish called reimen ("cold noodles"). Actually, the Korean original, called *naengmyeon*, uses buckwheat noodles. It's really up to you which to use; I like them both. Surprisingly, this is also really good with instant ramen, the kind you get for 75 cents a pack (though when I was a kid, they were 10 cents!). Prepared in a hot broth as directed, instant noodles tend to go soft and sad, but if you chill them in ice water when they're just cooked, they firm up nicely and retain a perfect bite.

This recipe is not quite Japanese, not quite Korean, but it is delicious—and simple. A mighty refreshing summer treat.

Yield:
4 servings

Ingredients:
6–6½ cups (1.4–1.5L) dashi, chilled
3 tbsp gochujang (Korean chili paste), tobanjian (Chinese chili-bean paste) or miso mixed with chili powder, to taste
1 tbsp soy sauce
1 tbsp rice vinegar
1 tbsp mirin
½ cucumber, seeds removed, julienned
½ apple or Asian pear, cored and julienned

Ingredients *continued*:
1¾ oz (about 50g) daikon or radishes, thinly sliced
1 tbsp rice vinegar
4 portions thin noodles
freshly ground black pepper
2 scallions, finely sliced
2 oz (60g) kimchi (optional, pages 32–33)
4 tsp garlic oil or sesame oil
4 boiled eggs, halved
1 tbsp sesame seeds
8–12 ice cubes
1 lime or lemon, cut into wedges

If you haven't got dashi already prepared and you're keen to make this, you can use dashi powder to make cold dashi in an instant. Simply dissolve the dashi powder in a little hot water in a bowl, then top it off with cold water. Mix the dashi with the gochujang, soy sauce, vinegar and mirin with a whisk until thoroughly blended. Taste and adjust the flavor as needed. Keep in the fridge until ready to serve. Toss the cucumber, apple or pear and daikon or radishes in vinegar. And now it is simply a matter of assembly.

Cook the noodles until al dente, drain and rinse them under cold running water to cool and to stop them from sticking together. Put the noodles into wide bowls and pour the cold dashi broth over, then top with the vinegared vegetables. Add the pepper, scallions and kimchi (if using). Drizzle the garlic or sesame oil around the broth and top each serving with the boiled egg halves and some sesame seeds. Lastly, add 2 or 3 ice cubes to each bowl. Serve with a wedge of lime or lemon.

Variations:
Use sticks of watermelon in place of the apple or pear, or use cucumber-chili ice cubes (pages 78–79) in place of plain ice.

Hiyashi Chūka

冷やし中華

(Ramen Salad)

This dish was developed by enterprising ramen shops to keep business steady during Kyushu's sweltering late summer months, when temperatures push 95°F and humidity can climb to 80%. Hardly the weather for burying your face in a cloud of hot pork fog, so instead there's *hiyashi chūka* ("chilled Chinese"), a sort of deconstructed ramen in salad form. It's like reimen (pages 190–191), but instead of a broth, it has a dressing—mine is made with sesame purée so it retains some of the creamy mouthfeel of hot ramen. Fantastic for lunch or a light dinner out in the garden. It is delicious with cold sake or cocktails, and is also very good picnic fodder for the two days of the year when that's an option in Britain.

Yield:

4 servings

Ingredients:

4 eggs
4 tsp soy sauce
4 tsp mirin
2 tbsp vegetable oil,
plus 1 tsp for the omelets
3 tbsp sesame seeds, *nerigoma*
sesame paste or tahini
2 tbsp sesame oil

Ingredients *continued*:

2 tbsp rice vinegar
2 tsp mustard
1 tsp sugar
4 portions medium-thick ramen noodles,
cooked al dente and chilled in ice water
3½ oz (100g) ham or cooked chicken,
cut into strips
½ cucumber, julienned or cut into strips
2 carrots, julienned or cut into strips
10–12 cherry tomatoes, cut into quarters
1½ oz (40g) beni shōga

Beat the eggs together with a teaspoon of the soy sauce and a teaspoon of the mirin. Heat 1 tsp oil in a nonstick frying pan and use a ladle or deep spoon to pour a very thin layer of egg into the pan, tilting it to cover the surface evenly. Cook for about a minute, then flip over and cook for another minute. Remove from the pan and set aside. Repeat until all the egg has been cooked and you have a short stack of thin omelets. Cut these into long strips about 1½ inches (4cm) wide, then again into small strips about ⅜ inch (1cm) across.

To make the dressing, if you're using whole sesame seeds, grind them in a mortar and pestle. Add a little of the sesame oil and keep grinding to form a buttery paste. Add the rest of the sesame oil and 2 tbsp vegetable oil, a little at a time, to emulsify. Transfer to a jar and add the remaining soy sauce and mirin and the vinegar, mustard and sugar. Shake hard to combine. If using nerigoma or tahini, simply put it in a bowl with the soy sauce, mirin, vinegar, mustard and sugar and stir well to combine.

To dress the salad, pile the ramen noodles in the center of a plate and arrange the ham or chicken, cucumber, carrots, egg strips and tomatoes around it in individual piles. Place the beni shōga in the center of the ramen. Pour on a few spoonfuls of dressing at the table.

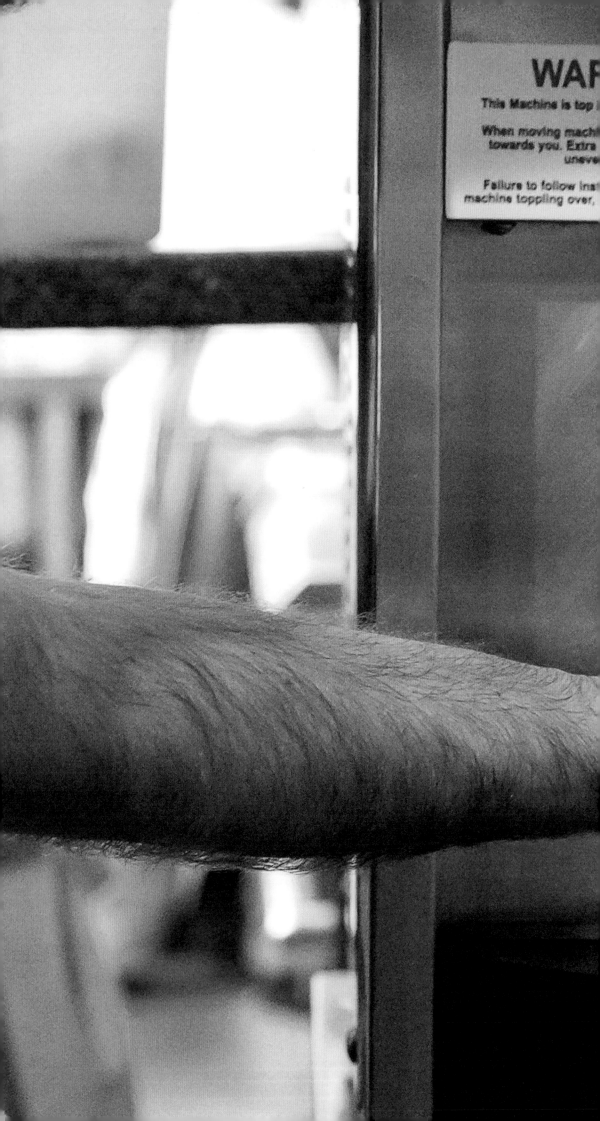

WAR

This Machine is top

When moving mach
towards you. Extra
uneve

Failure to follow ins
machine toppling over,

Desserts

デザート

It's often said that the Japanese aren't big on sweets. This isn't quite true—it's more accurate to say they aren't big on desserts, that is, a sweet grand finale to a meal. I've been treated so many times to extravagant multicourse feasts in Japan that have ended with an anticlimactic tablespoonful of sorbet and a wedge of fresh fruit. Japanese desserts are usually meant to refresh rather than sate or sedate.

That said, Japan is awash with fabulous, indulgent sweet things, but they're usually eaten as a snack, often in the afternoon, with tea or coffee. Look around in a Japanese department store food hall and you'll be dazzled by the array of both European and Japanese confections. Most urban train stations have a patisserie on the premises, not to mention a convenience store stocked with all sorts of candies, cakes and ice creams. Shopping mall food courts are also full of crepes, pastries and parfaits. And everywhere you turn, you'll find one of my favorite Japanese treats, soft-serve ice cream (pages 206–213).

Nagasaki Castella

長崎カステラ

In all honesty, I never really liked Nagasaki Castella, a kind of sponge cake whose ultimate ancestor is the Portuguese *pão-de-ló*, a.k.a. *pão de Castela*—"bread from Castile." It's essentially a pound cake, but it's a particularly dry and bland pound cake. So I've tweaked it, making it moister, lighter and more flavorful. Nagasaki natives would probably scratch their heads at this and say it isn't really Castella, but it's pretty close, and besides, deliciousness should never defer to authenticity.

Yield:
8–10 portions

Ingredients:
4 eggs, separated
11 tbsp (140g) sugar
1 cup (140g) bread flour
¼ tsp baking powder
½ tsp salt
3 tbsp (35g) milk
2 tbsp (35g) honey
2 tbsp (30g) melted unsalted butter
1 tsp vanilla extract
10 drops mandarin essential oil
  or 1 tsp orange extract

Preheat the oven to 350°F.

Whisk the egg whites in a clean bowl until light and frothy. Add the sugar, a little at a time, while whisking continuously, until stiff and glossy. Sift together the flour, baking powder and salt. Mix the milk, honey, butter, vanilla, mandarin oil and egg yolks together. Fold the liquid into the meringue, then fold in the flour, a bit at a time, until smooth.

Pour into a loaf pan lined with lightly greased parchment paper. Shake the pan and bang it firmly on the counter a few times to expel any large bubbles. Bake for 40 minutes, rotating the pan halfway through the cooking time. While still warm, tip the cake out upside down onto paper towels. Leave to cool, then trim and portion into neat rectangles. Serve with Whippy-san (pages 206–213) or whipped cream flavored with a spoonful of matcha (see pages 220–221).

Sātā Andaqī

サーターアンダギー

(Okinawan Doughnuts)

Sātā is "sugar" in Okinawan, and *andagī* means "fried." So there you go: deep-fried sugar! Sounds very American. But actually, these aren't that sweet, and they are denser and cakier than most doughnuts, similar to the fried dough buns found in mainland China. They have a lovely crunch, and they're a great showcase for Okinawan unrefined brown sugar or "black sugar." They go great with Whippy-san (pages 206–213), whipped cream or *kuromitsu* (below).

Yield:
about 20 doughnuts

Ingredients:
2 eggs
3⅓ tbsp (40g) dark muscovado sugar,
    dark brown sugar or molasses sugar
3 tbsp (40g) superfine sugar, plus 1½ tbsp
    (20g) more for dusting
1 tbsp (15g) unsalted butter, melted
1½ cups (200g) all-purpose flour
½ tsp baking powder
oil, for deep frying
about 3 tbsp (20g) kinako (soybean flour,
    see page 20)

Beat the eggs and sugars together until completely smooth and ribbony, then gradually drizzle in the melted butter (a stand mixer is useful here, if you have one). Sift in the flour and baking powder and mix together with a spatula; it should be stiff and sticky, like bread dough. Cover the batter with plastic wrap and let rest in the fridge for 30–60 minutes.

Heat the oil in a large, deep pan to 300–320°F. Use two spoons to form the batter into little quenelles or balls, and plop them into the oil. They'll puff up to about twice their size, so don't overcrowd the pan. Fry for 4–5 minutes, until a rich bronze color, then drain on paper towels and allow to cool. Combine the remaining superfine sugar and the kinako until well mixed. When the doughnuts are no longer hot to the touch, roll in the kinako sugar.

Kuromitsu

黒蜜

(Black Sugar Syrup)

Kuromitsu is sold in squeezy bottles in Japan, like honey, and is drizzled over all sorts of sweets, from mochi to ice cream. I think it's delicious with Castella (pages 196–197), Whippy-san (pages 206–207) or *sātā andagī* (above). You can also use ordinary molasses in its place, although that's a little more intense than what you'd get in Japan.

Yield:
about 1¼ cups (300ml)

Ingredients:
¾ cup (175ml) water
1¼ cups (250g) dark muscovado sugar,
    dark brown sugar or molasses sugar

Combine the water and sugar in a saucepan and bring to a simmer, stirring to make sure all the sugar is dissolved. Transfer to a jar and leave to cool before using. Keeps in the cupboard for ages.

Mojiko Roll Cake
門司港ロールケーキ

Along with yaki-curry (pages 90–91), one of Mojiko's more dubious specialties is the roll cake—that is, a Swiss roll or jelly roll. You can even buy them at the Kitakyushu airport. But as far as I can tell, they have little to do with the actual produce of Mojiko. I fill mine with banana custard, in keeping with Mojiko's history as Japan's banana gateway.

Yield:
10–12 servings

Ingredients:

For the banana crème:
1 sheet gelatin
1 very ripe banana
⅓ cup (70ml) whole milk
6⅓ tbsp (80g) sugar
¼ tsp salt
1 tbsp cornstarch
2 egg yolks
6½ tbsp (100ml) heavy cream
2 tsp (10g) butter, melted
juice of ½ lemon
3¾ tbsp (30g) confectioners' sugar
¼ tsp yellow food coloring

For the cake:
4 egg whites
6⅓ tbsp (80g) sugar
6 egg yolks
1 tbsp liquid glucose (glucose syrup)
¼ cup (40g) black sesame purée
   (neri-kurogoma) or black sesame seeds
   ground as finely as possible
2 tbsp black sesame seeds
1 tsp black food coloring (optional)
⅓ cup (40g) all-purpose flour
2¾ tbsp (40g) unsalted butter, melted
5⅓ oz (150g) fresh fruit, such as strawberries,
   melon or satsuma oranges, cut into
   small pieces

For the banana crème:
Soak the gelatin in cold water. Purée the banana with the milk in a blender until smooth. Add to a saucepan with the sugar and salt and bring to a simmer. Whisk together the cornstarch and egg yolks to form a paste, and whisk in a little of the hot banana mixture to temper. Pour the yolks into 2 tbsp (30ml) of the cream, stir to combine, then pour into the hot banana mixture and continue to cook on a medium heat, stirring constantly, until the custard thickens. Whisk in the softened gelatin, butter and lemon juice and pour into a bowl to cool and set—to prevent a skin from forming on the custard press some plastic wrap or parchment to its surface. When the custard is completely cold, beat the remaining 4½ tbsp (70ml) cream along with the confectioners' sugar and food coloring to firm peaks and fold into the banana custard.

For the cake:
Preheat the oven to 400°F. Make a meringue from the egg whites and half the sugar: in a clean bowl, beat the egg whites until fluffy, then gradually add half the sugar and continue to beat until stiff peaks form. Cream the remaining sugar with the egg yolks and liquid glucose with an electric mixer until smooth and pale, then stir in the neri-kurogoma, the black sesame seeds and the food coloring (if using). Fold the meringue and the yolk mixture together and add the flour and melted butter. Stir to combine. Pour into a lined and lightly greased rimmed baking sheet and bake for 10–12 minutes. Leave to cool before filling and rolling.

Spread the banana crème into a thick, even layer along the surface of the sponge cake. Distribute the chopped fruit evenly on top of the crème. Roll it up away from you, with a tea towel underneath, if need be, to keep it even. Once rolled, wrap carefully but tightly in plastic wrap and place in the fridge or freezer to firm up. Slice and serve with more fresh fruit, if you like.

Strawberry Daifuku
イチゴ大福

(Strawberry and Red Bean Paste Mochi Dumplings)

This is a popular, classic tea confection eaten throughout Japan, but especially prized in Fukuoka prefecture because of its fields of big, sweet strawberries. These little dumplings are a study in textures: chewy mochi, rich red bean paste and juicy strawberries. Like most traditional Japanese desserts, they aren't that sweet, and they're actually sort of healthy. You can get store-bought sweet red bean paste to make this easier, but it will also make it more expensive.

Yield:
6 daifuku

Ingredients:
For the red bean paste:
3½ oz (100g) dried adzuki beans
½ cup (100g) superfine sugar

For the mochi:
1 cup (150g) glutinous rice flour (shiratamako or mochiko)
4½ tbsp confectioners' sugar
⅝ cup (150ml) water

To assemble:
6 large strawberries, hulled
cornstarch or potato flour, as needed

For the red bean paste:
Soak the adzuki beans in water overnight. Drain and then place them in a saucepan or pressure cooker with water to cover. Boil until the beans are very tender—you should be able to crush them easily between your fingers. This should take about 20 minutes in a pressure cooker or 1 hour in a saucepan. Top off with water as needed, but in the end let the pan boil dry (stirring to make sure the beans don't stick). Mash in the sugar, and then pass the mixture through a sieve so you have a perfectly smooth paste. Chill in the refrigerator until needed.

For the mochi:
Combine the rice flour and sugar in a heatproof bowl. Add a third of the water and stir to combine, add another third and stir again, then add the remaining water and stir until the mixture is smooth and glossy. Place the bowl in a steamer and steam for 15 minutes. Remove the mochi from the bowl with a spatula and dust lightly with cornstarch or potato flour.

To assemble:
Cut the mochi into 6 equal pieces and divide the bean paste into 6 balls. Rub your hands with a little cornstarch to keep them from getting sticky, and gently wrap the bean paste around the strawberries so they're evenly coated—like putting sausage meat around a Scotch egg. Flatten each ball of mochi with your hands or a rolling pin, using a little cornstarch to keep it from sticking, but don't overdo it; you need them to be a little sticky to seal the dumplings. Cup a round of mochi in the palm of your hand, then place the bean-coated strawberry inside, pointed end down. Draw up the sides of the dough to cover the strawberry and pinch it together to seal on the bottom. Repeat with the remaining strawberries. Handling the bean-coated strawberries can be tricky; to make it easier, put them in the freezer for about 30 minutes to firm up before wrapping them in the mochi.

DESSERTS

Matcha Marubōlo

抹茶丸ボー口

Marubōlo is a funny hybrid word that simply means "round cookie," using the Japanese word for "circle" (*maru*) and the Portuguese word for "cookie" (*bolo*). A staple souvenir from Saga prefecture, these are typically flavored only with soy sauce and honey, and you could make them like that, but I add matcha (see pages 220–221) because I like it. I describe the texture as a cross between a *macaron* shell and a cupcake top. Firm yet soft and chewy. These are really nice as a sandwich cookie filled with matcha buttercream (below).

Yield:
30 cookies

Ingredients:
2½ cups (300g) all-purpose flour
1 tsp baking soda
1 tsp baking powder
½ oz (15g) matcha

Ingredients *continued*:
1 cup (200g) superfine sugar, plus extra
    for dusting
½ tsp sesame oil
1 tsp honey
3 eggs
1 tsp soy sauce
unsalted butter, melted

Combine the flour, baking soda, baking powder and matcha. Whisk together the sugar, oil, honey, eggs and soy sauce in a separate bowl. Sift in the dry ingredients and stir to combine. The dough should be quite stiff but still sticky. Wrap the dough in plastic wrap and rest in the fridge for 30–60 minutes.

Preheat the oven to 350°F. Fill a bowl with water to dampen your hands. Line 2 baking sheets with parchment paper and lightly grease or butter them. Use a dessert spoon to portion the dough and use your hands to roll it into balls. Place the balls at least 1½ inches (4cm) apart on the prepared baking sheets and bake for about 11 minutes, until just barely starting to brown. While the cookies bake, melt some butter in a pan. As soon as the cookies come out of the oven, brush them with a little melted butter and dust generously with superfine sugar.

Matcha Buttercream

抹茶バタークリーム

This is a great way to enhance both marubōlo and Castella—or just plain cupcakes.

Yield:
17½ oz (500g)

Ingredients:
⅔ cup (150g) unsalted butter, at room
    temperature
2½ cups (300g) confectioners' sugar
2 tbsp milk
1 tsp vanilla extract or the seeds of
    1 vanilla bean (optional)
⅓ oz (10g) matcha

Use a handheld or stand mixer to blend together the butter and sugar. Add the milk to loosen it, then add the vanilla (if using) and matcha. Cover and keep at room temperature until ready to use.

Whippy-san
ホイッピーさん

(Japanese Mr. Whippy)

In the UK and the US, soft-serve ice cream usually comes in one, maybe two flavors if you're lucky: chocolate and vanilla. Ho hum. But in Japan they have as many flavors as colors of the rainbow! Often they'll incorporate some prized local ingredient, and in my travels I've encountered (to name a few) purple sweet potato, pumpkin, black sesame, red bean, white bean, black bean, yuzu, cantaloupe, Camembert, soy sauce, sea urchin, almond, white peach and bitter chocolate. There really are no bounds to what you can make into soft-serve. In Japan it's simply called "soft cream," but I call it "Whippy-san"—Japanese Mr. Whippy.

Whippy-san Base

プレーンホイッピーさん

There are a couple of different ways to achieve the light, lickably soft texture of Whippy-san at home (as actual Mr. Whippy machines cost thousands of dollars and weigh more than I do, that option is probably not on the table for most of you). One is to simply churn the ice cream in an ice cream maker until soft-set, and serve immediately. The other is to put the churned ice cream into a piping bag, set it in the freezer, then let it thaw slightly in the fridge until it becomes workable and pipe it out.

My Whippy-san recipe uses cornstarch rather than eggs to thicken and stabilize, because (a) making an egg custard is a pain in the ass, (b) cornstarch is cheaper than egg yolks, (c) eggs can make your ice cream taste eggy and (d) it adds more structure to the ice cream, preventing crystallization and allowing you to thaw and refreeze it without as much detriment to the texture. There is also a little bit of liquor in the base; this lowers the freezing temperature, so it doesn't get rock hard in the freezer and is more scoopable when you take it out.

This is the base recipe for the different flavor recipes that follow. With all of these Whippy-san recipes, you should let the mixture get nice and cold in the fridge before processing in an ice cream maker so you get a smooth and even end product.

Yield:
3½–3¾ cups (850–900ml), about 8 scoops

Ingredients:
3 tbsp cornstarch
2¼ cups (500ml) whole milk
1¼ cups (300ml) heavy cream
½ cup (100g) superfine sugar
2 tbsp orange liqueur, rum, brandy or vodka—any booze you like, really, as long as its flavor isn't too strong (e.g., Highland whisky)

Stir the cornstarch together with about ¼ cup (60ml) of the milk to form a smooth paste. Heat the remaining milk, cream and sugar together in a large, deep saucepan until it comes to the boil, then reduce the heat to a low simmer. Whisk in the milk and cornstarch mixture, little by little, and cook for about 5 minutes, until it is thick like custard and no longer floury on the palate. Pass through a fine sieve, then stir in the liquor, cover and refrigerate until needed.

Sweet Potato Whippy-san

薩摩芋ホイッピーさん

Maybe it's because I grew up on pumpkin pie, but I simply adore sweet potato in desserts—the clue is in the name. They're rich, fruity and naturally creamy, so they make a great ice cream, as I discovered in Kyushu, where it's so popular that Häagen-Dazs even released their own version. In Chinatown I occasionally find wonderful purple-fleshed sweet potatoes, which give this ice cream a striking, otherworldly color. If you happen upon them, snatch them up. But normal orange sweet potatoes will be just as tasty.

Yield:
3⅓–3¾ cups (800–900ml),
about 8 scoops

Ingredients:
14–17½ oz (400–500g) sweet potatoes, peeled and cut into chunks
1 tbsp vegetable oil
½ cup (100g) superfine sugar or light brown sugar
½ batch Whippy-san base (pages 206–207)

Preheat the oven to 350°F. Toss the prepared sweet potatoes in the oil and spread out evenly on a baking sheet. Bake for about 40 minutes or until very soft. Purée with the sugar while still hot. You can leave it a little chunky for extra texture, or pass the purée through a sieve to make it perfectly smooth—totally up to you. Mix the purée into the Whippy-san base. Chill, then process according to your ice cream maker's instructions.

Shichimi Chocolate Whippy-san
七味チョコレートホイッピーさん

My take on the classic chili and chocolate combo uses shichimi, which contributes more than just heat; it's got orange zest for a nice aroma and tang as well as a small amount of seaweed, which gives a rich, subtly savory character.

Yield:
2 cups (450ml), about 4 scoops

Ingredients:
½ batch Whippy-san base (pages 206–207)
2¾ oz (80g) dark chocolate
2 tsp shichimi

Heat the Whippy-san base to a simmer and whisk in the chocolate and shichimi. When the chocolate is completely melted, chill, then process according to your ice cream maker's instructions.

Miso Caramel Whippy-san
味噌キャラメルホイッピーさん

A combination so good, I wonder why Ben & Jerry's hasn't snatched it up and released it under some stupid hippie name—"Give Miso Chance," perhaps. Anyway, it's fabulous: basically like salted caramel with additional fruity-nutty-malty notes. It also works pretty well with 1½–2 tablespoons of soy sauce in place of the miso.

Yield:
3½ cups (750ml), about 7 scoops

Ingredients:
9½ tbsp (120g) superfine sugar
1 tbsp water
⅝ cup (150ml) whole milk
3 tbsp (55g) miso
½ tsp vanilla extract
½ batch Whippy-san base (pages 206–207)

Put the sugar and 1 tablespoon of the water in a large saucepan over a gentle heat and cook slowly until the sugar has all dissolved and you have a dark amber caramel (don't worry if the sugar starts to crystallize; just stir well and break up any chunks with your spoon until they dissolve). Meanwhile, in another saucepan, heat the milk to a simmer. Whisk the hot milk into the caramel—this will bubble up quite a lot. Keep whisking to make sure all the caramel has dissolved into the milk. Remove from the heat and whisk in the miso and vanilla, making sure the miso is completely dissolved and there are no chunks left. Whisk in the Whippy-san base, then pass the mixture through a sieve. Chill, then process according to your ice cream maker's instructions.

Hōjicha Whippy-san
焙じ茶ホイッピーさん

(Roasted Green Tea Mr. Whippy)

Hōjicha has some of the fresh, grassy notes of green tea, but with a distinct caramel-walnut flavor from being lightly dry-roasted. It makes a beautiful ice cream, especially nice in autumn. You can also use oolong or a similar Chinese black tea, or even matcha—a modern classic.

Yield:
2 cups (450ml), about 4 scoops

Ingredients:
about 1½ tbsp (6g) loose-leaf hōjicha
½ batch Whippy-san base (pages 206–207)

Stir the hōjicha into the Whippy-san base and bring to a simmer. Remove from the heat and leave to infuse for 5–10 minutes. Pass the mixture through a fine sieve. Chill, then process according to your ice cream maker's instructions.

White Peach Whippy-san
白桃ホイッピーさん

Peaches and cream, Japanese-style. A beautiful late summer treat that you can enjoy well into the autumn—it keeps for several months in the freezer. If you're making this, I'd recommend a little umeshu (plum wine—see pages 224–225) as the liquor in your Whippy-san base. The flavors match perfectly. Mirabelle or peach schnapps is nice too.

Yield:
3½ cups (750ml), about 7 scoops

Ingredients:
2 ripe white peaches or nectarines,
   stones removed, roughly chopped
½ batch Whippy-san base (pages 206–207)

Add the peaches to the Whippy-san base in a saucepan and bring to a simmer. Remove from the heat, then purée the mixture with an immersion blender or in a food processor and pass through a fine sieve. Chill, then process according to your ice cream maker's instructions.

Kinako Whippy-san

きな粉ホイッピーさん

(Soybean Flour Mr. Whippy)

Who'd have thought soybean flour could be so rich, nutty and indulgent? The Japanese, that's who. This Whippy-san recipe is one of my personal favorites.

Yield:
3½–3¾ cups (850–900ml), about 8 scoops

Ingredients:
¾ cup (80g) kinako (soybean flour, see page 20)
2¼ cups (500ml) whole milk
1¼ cups (300ml) heavy cream
½ cup (100g) superfine sugar
2 tbsp mellow-flavored alcohol of your choice

Stir the kinako together with ¼ cup (60ml) of the milk to form a smooth paste. Heat the remaining milk together with the cream and sugar in a large, deep saucepan until it comes to the boil, then reduce the heat to a low simmer.

Whisk in the kinako paste, little by little, until well combined. Continue to cook over a very low heat for about 5 minutes, or until the mixture thickens to a custard-like consistency. Pass the mixture through a fine sieve, then stir in the liquor. Cover and leave to cool. Refrigerate to chill completely before processing according to your ice cream maker's instructions.

Drinks
飲み物

Beverages of Southern Japan:
A Field Guide

A commonly heard expression at izakaya and restaurants in Japan is "toriaezu, beer," meaning "first of all, beer." This sets the tone for a typical evening out: first, a drink to unwind and relax, to loosen your tie, undo your top button and drop some of the formalities that dominate Japanese working life. Having that first drink is like crossing a threshold from work to play.

The word izakaya is often translated as something like "Japanese pub" or "Japanese tapas bar," which does convey its casual, communal atmosphere, but I prefer the literal translation: "place to stay and drink." Originally they were sake shops that let their customers drink on the premises, and over time they started serving snacks to accompany the liquor. This is important: the izakaya experience is as much about drinking as it is about eating. And rightly so!

Beer is easily the most popular beverage, especially before and during a meal. But there is a wealth of other drinks available at most izakaya, from the classic sake to Western-style cocktails to the distinctly southern (but nationally popular) spirit called shochu. This is a guide to some of Kyushu's and Okinawa's most common drinks, with some suggestions on how to serve and pair them with food.

Beer
ビール

Most beer consumed in Japan is fizzy yellow lager—you've probably had Kirin, Asahi or Sapporo, which for more than a century have been the three dominant brands. These are really not far off your garden-variety, mass-produced continental lager (indeed, the versions found in the UK are actually brewed under contract in Europe or North America). I do think they're a little cleaner and crisper than their European counterparts, but that may just be nostalgia talking. They often use rice in place of some of the malt, which gives the beer a very light and dry quality. There's not much to say about them, except that because they're so plain and easy to drink, they work fine with most izakaya foods. Their sparkling mouthfeel and snappy finish act as a good palate cleanser between mouthfuls of rich, porky dishes like Hakata ramen (pages 172–173) or gyoza (pages 60–61). They're also a pleasant counterpart for snacky, salty dishes like chicken skin skewers (pages 136–137) or karashi renkon (pages 74–75).

Less common is what's called ji-beer, meaning "local beer"—basically the same as what we know as craft beer or microbrewed beer. But these more flavorful beers are increasingly popular and are starting to make inroads onto izakaya drink menus. Because Japan has always borrowed its brewing techniques and methods from abroad and built on them using indigenous ingredients and ideas, the range of flavors

found from these breweries can be quite broad. Any given micro-brewery could produce a Czech-style pilsner, a German wheat beer, an English porter, and then something distinctly Japanese, like a yuzu pale ale. Ji-beer is quite expensive in Japan and astronomically expensive in the UK and US (if you can get it), so I'd recommend good British, European or American craft beer as an alternative. These are not as universally compatible with izakaya food as Japanese lagers, but the right match can make for a very exciting flavor experience. Try a Belgian witbier with kake-ae (pages 52–53), an American IPA with champloo (pages 88–89) or an English bitter with chicken nanban (pages 100–101). I've worked with an East London brewery called Pressure Drop to create two of our own Nanban beers, both designed for optimum compatability with the food. One is a light, dry sweet potato ale, and the other a highly aromatic wheat IPA with yuzu, orange and grapefruit.

Shochu
焼酎

The distilled spirit shochu is without question the drink most commonly associated with Kyushu. Because in the past distillation technology was rarely used in Japan, it was once known as a drink for the upper classes, and is actually mentioned as a restorative salve for wounds in samurai legends. But over time, distillation and therefore shochu became more common. Also, it could be made from barley or potatoes as opposed to rice, which was considered more desirable and luxurious, so shochu's reputation dropped and it became known as a vaguely lower-class, old-fashioned and generally inferior drink.

However, a variety of factors over the course of the 20th century ushered in a shochu boom, and in 2003 it surpassed sake in domestic shipments. In Kyushu, shochu had been more popular for many decades, in part due to the area's long history of growing sweet potatoes, one of its key ingredients. In fact, the word *sake*, which actually just means "liquor," is often taken to mean shochu in Kyushu bars—if you want what we know as sake, you'll have to order it by its more specific name, *Nihon-shu* (Japanese liquor).

Shochu is either single distilled, or multiple distilled and then diluted, so its strength is usually around 25%—less than most spirits, but still up there. It can be produced in many different ways, from many different ingredients, but these are some of the more common:

——— *Imo* (potato): sweet potato shochu is prized for its fruity-earthy flavor, reminiscent of nuts or overripe fruit. Kagoshima and Miyazaki prefectures are especially famous for their extensive varieties.

——— *Mugi* (barley or wheat): barley tends to ferment a bit cleaner than sweet potato, making the resultant shochu more like a mellow vodka in terms of flavor.

——— *Kome* (rice): this classic shochu recalls some of the floral-sweet flavors of sake. The prefectures of Saga and rural Kumamoto, with their milder climates and good rice, produce some of Kyushu's best.

There are all kinds of other fermentables used in shochu production, including buckwheat, unrefined sugar, sesame seeds, chestnuts—I've even had one distilled from sweet potato's stuck-up cousin, carrot (it was nice). Another key ingredient that determines the ultimate flavor of a shochu is the mold (*kōji*) used during production. There are dozens of strains, but the main ones are classified as white (*shiro*), black (*kuro*) or red (*aka*). White tends to be more neutral and crisp; black is rich and nutty; red is fruity and tangy. But these are just general guidelines; the truth is, flavors vary even among shochu made from the same base fermentable and the same mold. The real way to learn about shochu is to get yourself a couple of bottles and start drinking! These are some of my favorite shochu available in the UK and US:

——— Kuro Kirishima: this black kōji sweet potato shochu from Miyazaki has a complex but easy-drinking flavor of almonds, melon and a hint of peaty smoke. It's a great introductory shochu if you're a fan of single-malt whisky or dry sherry, with a richness that works beautifully with hearty dishes like tonkotsu ramen (pages 150–151) or beef with hot mustard (page 131). Deliriously relaxing when served with hot water.

——— Unkai: also from Miyazaki, this is a buckwheat shochu that is one of the cleanest-tasting around. It's mostly neutral but with very faint floral and nutty notes, perfect for mixed drinks. Crisp and refreshing, it's fabulous with tempura (pages 96–97) or hiyajiru (pages 78–79).

——— Ginza no Suzume: from Oita, this delicious barley shochu is sweet and delicate with hints of citrus, good for mixing or drinking on the rocks. There is also a version aged in bourbon barrels (*Kōhaku*), which gives a light caramel/Brazil-nut flavor and smooths it out to the point of dangerous drinkability. With plenty of ice, it's an exquisite mouth-mellower alongside ramen or kara-age (pages 64–65).

——— Kannoko: I avoided this shochu for years because it's inexpensive and has an ugly label. Unwise! It is now a go-to shochu. A Kagoshima shochu made from barley and aged in oak barrels for three years, it has a remarkably pronounced banana aroma and smooth, sweet flavor. Perfect for yaki-curry (pages 90–91) or with desserts like Castella (pages 196–197) or miso-caramel Mr. Whippy ice cream (page 210).

Shochu can be drunk neat, on ice, with cold water or with hot water (*oyuwari*). Or it can be enjoyed with soda and flavored syrups, as in chu-hi (pages 234–237).

Tea
お茶

Japan runs on tea. It's omnipresent—at home, at the office, in convenience stores, in vending machines and at the izakaya. So if you're having lunch or aren't imbibing for some silly reason, tea is the way to go. There are countless varieties, of course, but the main ones you'll find served alongside casual fare are *sencha*, *oolong* and *mugicha*. Sencha is a dried, whole-leaf Japanese green tea and is usually light and grassy and a little umami. Like sake, it's good with just about anything, especially tofu and dashi-based dishes. Oolong is richer, toastier, more tannic and fruitier, and is said to help aid digestion, but I don't know if that's true. I like it with Chinese-inflected dishes like buta kakuni manjū (pages 56–57). And mugicha isn't actually tea at all, but an infusion of toasted barley kernels, malty and caramelly yet dry. It's a noodle shop staple, often provided free of charge, and it's also great with Korean-influenced spicy recipes like kimchi (pages 32–33).

You may also find matcha at izakaya, though this is usually more the domain of dedicated tea rooms and high-end restaurants. Matcha is an intensely flavored, powdered green tea. Its flavor is grassy and floral, astringent yet sweet. Think of it as the espresso of green tea: its strong taste and vibrant green color make it a staple flavoring for all manner of Japanese sweets. It's especially good with fatty preparations like buttercream or with whipped cream, which help round off its rough edges.

Awamori
泡盛

Awamori is shochu's rambunctious island cousin, the spirit of Okinawa. More closely related to Chinese liquor, awamori actually has its origins in Thailand, and still uses long-grain rice as its fermentable—unusual for Japanese drinks. (Of course, like many things Okinawan, its Japaneseness is questionable.) It's often stronger and more floral than shochu, anywhere from 25–50% ABV, and it marries well with most Okinawan dishes, especially tonpi (pages 58–59). Awamori is best served straight or on the rocks.

Sake
日本酒

Sake is—in theory at least—the national drink of Japan, hence its proper name, Nihon-shu: Japanese liquor. But in practice, it's less popular than beer or shochu, especially in Kyushu, but that doesn't mean it hasn't a place at the southern izakaya table. The details of sake (and there are many) are better covered elsewhere, as in Philip Harper's excellent *The Book of Sake*. I will say that it is worth spending a little extra money on sake. It's not like wine; a decent bottle cannot be had for under $15, and actually you start to see the best value around $30. A saying among sake enthusiasts in Japan is "food and sake do not fight," and this is true—sake tends to mingle with most Japanese dishes beautifully, partly due to its clean, balanced nature. With the Nanban style of Japanese soul food, I like dry, aromatic varieties; I particularly love *kimoto* or *yamahai* sake, which ferment with a higher quantity of lactobacillus and other wild bacteria, giving the end result an acidic, rustic character—think yogurt, hard cider and sourdough bread. These are really special with sour, fishy or funky dishes like motsu nabe (pages 108–109), mentaiko pasta (pages 86–87) and nanban-zuke (pages 104–105).

But I also have a real love for classically refined sake, especially with more delicate recipes. These usually fall under the category of *junmai* (all-rice), *ginjō* (highly polished rice) or *daiginjō* (very highly polished rice)—note that not all ginjō and daiginjō are junmai, and vice versa. But if you choose a sake with any of these designations, you're likely to get a light, dry, balanced and fruity sake. Try these with nadōfu (pages 70–71). In terms of how to drink it, there is a widespread misunderstanding that sake should be served hot. This is generally true of rougher, earthier sake (or if it's cold outside), but actually most sake is at its best lightly chilled, like white wine. These days many sake bottles are now outfitted with very useful English labels with tasting notes as well as recommendations for serving temperature, which helps take the guesswork out of enjoying your undoubtedly expensive sake.

Whisky
ウィスキー

Japanese whisky has cultivated a deservedly excellent reputation abroad. The higher-end bottles, such as the Yamazaki and Hakushu malts, are simply exquisite and are best sipped on their own, accompanied only by Miles Davis and furtive flirting. But ordinary, bottom-shelf whisky has its place in Japan as well, especially at the izakaya; a whisky highball, all dry and fizzy and tangy, works much like lager as an all-purpose palate cleanser. They've become so popular in Japan that some bars now serve them premixed on draught.

Wine
ワイン

Bah! I hate wine. I don't really, but I do hate that it has come to completely dominate the world of food. Not everything has to go with wine! Sometimes other drinks are simply a better match—I want *ale*, not claret, with my steak and *ale* pie, thank you very much. And in the case of southern Japanese food, it'll be beer, shochu or sake. It's not unusual for izakaya in Japan not to offer wine at all, and if they do, it's often just two options: white or red. And that's as far as I'll go with wine recommendations: red for meaty dishes like the Sasebo burger (pages 118–119); white for lighter fare like satsuma-age (pages 66–67). Many of you will have far more wine knowledge than I; I'll leave the specifics to you and your more-educated experimentation.

Liqueurs
リキュール

Fruity alcohol liqueurs are popular in Japan, from European standards like crème de cassis and curaçao to Japanese inventions like *yuzu-shu* and the classic *umeshu*—plum wine. Umeshu is an infusion of unripe Japanese plums (actually more like apricots) in clear spirit with sugar, resulting in a delicious, smooth, sweet-and-sour liqueur. Topped up with soda, it's a good aperitif, and on the rocks, it's a good dessert option alongside ice cream or Castella (pages 206–213 and 196–197).

Cocktails
カクテル

Cocktail culture in Japan is very interesting. Izakaya (as well as karaoke joints, bars and nightclubs) usually have a well-stocked liquor shelf and a substantial cocktail menu, although they tend to feature drinks that are somewhat old-fashioned by British bar standards: things like Campari soda, kir, Moscow mules and gin rickeys are not uncommon. Many also combine European liquors with popular Japanese soft drinks like oolong tea or Calpis, a fizzy Yakult-like beverage. The only rule of izakaya cocktail lists seems to be "anything goes," though highballs and long drinks (served in tall glasses with more ice and mixer than alcohol) are generally favored over short drinks like martinis or manhattans. For Nanban I've developed a tight list of cocktails (pages 226–237) that combine classic cocktail recipes with Kyushu flavors. They're better for drinking before or after the meal, but the Kyushu Libre (page 231) works well in place of beer, or the Go! Go! Gimlet (pages 232–233) instead of sake or white wine.

Nanhattan

ナンハッタン

The manhattan is my favorite cocktail. It's a bit like Michael Caine: timeless and classy, but also cheeky and a little rough around the edges. When I was putting together Nanban's cocktail menu, I knew a variant of the manhattan had to be on there. But I wanted to keep the flavors true while giving it a distinctly southern Japanese twang.

Using Japanese whisky was an obvious choice. Not just because it would establish a Japanese theme, but because the flavors in most Japanese whiskies just work—they tend to be subtle and smooth but still full of verve and character, like old leather-bound books. Once that was established, I started thinking about the drink's other elements: vermouth and bitters. How could I introduce a noticeably Kyushu flavor to them without disrupting the classic cocktail's perfect balance?

The answer, of course, is citrus. Not exuberant yuzu or puckering lemon, but something sweeter and more approachable: good ol' orange. Kyushu is an absolute paradise of oranges, from the bright and aromatic satsuma to the candy-like *dekopon*. And since orange peel is already a typical garnish for the manhattan, there's a precedent for it. In my "Nanhattan," that orange note comes in three forms: peel, bitters and vermouth. I also added a tiny bit of shochu for its Kyushu character and earthy-fruity aroma. The result is warmingly familiar yet subtly exotic. And it is delightfully, dangerously drinkable.

Yield:
about 2¼ cups (500ml)

For the tangerine vermouth:
2¼ cups (500ml) white (dry) vermouth
1 tangerine, washed and cut
into small chunks

Yield:
makes 1 drink

For the Nanhattan:
3¼ tbsp (50ml) Japanese whisky
1 tbsp (15ml) tangerine vermouth,
or 2 tsp (10ml) dry vermouth and 1 tsp
(5ml) orange liqueur
1 tbsp (15ml) shochu (use aged shochu
if you can)
1–2 dashes orange bitters (available at good
liquor stores or online)
strip of orange peel, trimmed of any white pith

For the tangerine vermouth:
Place the white vermouth and the tangerine in an air-tight bottle or jar (I just use the vermouth bottle after drinking a third of it). Give it a shake and leave to infuse at room temperature for 1–4 weeks, shaking it vigorously whenever you think of it.

For the Nanhattan:
When ready to serve, chill your cocktail glass with ice water or by sticking it in the freezer. Pour the whisky, tangerine vermouth, shochu and bitters into a cocktail shaker or jar with ice. Stir or shake for a minute or so. Strain into your chilled glass. Twist the orange peel above the glass and wipe it around the rim, then drop it into the cocktail. Serve, enjoy, relax and have some kushiyaki (pages 122–141).

Miyazaki Mai Tai
宮崎マイタイ

Raise your hand if you think mai tais are big, pink, sweet, pineappley and garnished with canned fruit threaded onto a tiny parasol. Okay, now sheepishly put your hand down and listen up: the classic mai tai in no way resembles the many terrifying, oversweet, Technicolor versions found in crappy bars and resorts around the world. It is almost pure booze, deliciously tart and intriguingly aromatic. It's one of my favorites, so the fact that it is so bastardized with things like coconut rum, grenadine and canned pineapple juice is a source of great ire to me.

Trader Vic's original 1934 recipe calls for five ingredients, only one of which is fruit juice—and it's lime. My Japanized version, named and flavored with Miyazaki prefecture in mind, stays true to the overall flavor of the original with just a few flourishes.

Yield:

makes 1 drink

Ingredients:
2½ tbsp (40ml) shochu (or white rum)
1 tbsp (15ml) orange liqueur (triple sec)
1 tbsp (15ml) yuzu or lime juice
1 tbsp (15ml) orgeat syrup
   (available online or at good liquor stores)
2 tsp (10ml) simple syrup
   (1 tsp sugar dissolved into 1 tsp hot water, cooled)
ice cubes, to serve
2 tsp (10ml) dark/spiced rum (optional)
slice of lime, to garnish

Combine everything except the dark rum (if using) in a cocktail shaker or jar with ice, seal and shake well until everything is very cold. Pour into a tumbler of ice and then pour the dark rum (if using) over so it floats on top. Garnish with a slice of lime. Tiny parasol strictly optional.

Variation:
Use tangerine vermouth (page 227) in place of the orgeat syrup.

Sakurajima Sunrise

桜島日の出

Sakurajima ("cherry blossom island") is a massive volcano in Kagoshima Bay, but its imposing presence is more serene than explosive. The smoke and ash rising from its caldera create mesmerizingly beautiful sunsets—or sunrises, if you're up early for a dip in a hot spring.

I like tequila and I like orange juice. And I like grenadine, too, but for some reason the tequila sunrise has never really charmed me as a cocktail. I think it's a bit too candy-sweet and a bit bland. I've tweaked it to incorporate southern Japanese flavors and make it a little sharper and stronger. The color is less vivid than the classic version, but that's okay—it still has an appealing, soft gradient.

Yield:
makes 1 drink

Ingredients:
5 tsp (25ml) tequila
5 tsp (25ml) shochu
5⅓ tbsp (80ml) orange juice
juice of 1 lime
ice cubes, to serve
1 tbsp (15ml) umeshu
slice of orange, to garnish

Pour the tequila, shochu, orange juice and lime juice into a tumbler or highball glass with ice. Pour in the umeshu slowly, so the colors don't mix completely. Garnish with a slice of orange.

Kyushu Libre
九州リブレ

This is simply a southern Japanese twist on the fabulous Cuba libre. There's a touch of yuzu and chili to bring this into barbarian territory.

Yield:
about 1⅔ cups (400ml)

For the yuzu-koshō syrup:
3¼ tbsp (50ml) yuzu juice
1 tsp chopped green chili
2 tsp grated fresh ginger
½ lime, chopped
6⅓ tbsp (80g) sugar
6½ tbsp (100ml) water
1 tsp yuzu-koshō

Yield:
makes 1 drink

For the Kyushu Libre:
5 tsp (25ml) shochu
5 tsp (25ml) dark rum
1 tbsp (15ml) yuzu-koshō syrup
ice cubes, to serve
⅞ cup (200ml) cola
slice of lime, to garnish

For the yuzu-koshō syrup:
Purée all the syrup ingredients in a blender. Pour into a jar or bottle, seal, refrigerate and leave to infuse for at least 1 day and for up to 4 weeks.

For the Kyushu Libre:
Pour the shochu, rum and syrup into a long glass. Fill with ice and top with cola. Garnish with a slice of lime.

Go! Go! Gimlet
ゴーゴーギムレット

I recently rediscovered the gimlet, and I had to wonder why it has fallen out of fashion. It's gin, it's lime—it's delicious! This Kyushu-ized recipe is named after my favorite band from Kagoshima, Go!Go! 7188 (nope, I don't know what it means) and features shochu and yuzu-koshō to give it a brash southern twang.

Yield:	Ingredients:
makes 1 drink	5 tsp (25ml) gin
	5 tsp (25ml) shochu
	1 tbsp (15ml) yuzu-koshō syrup (pages 230–231)
	ice cubes, to serve
	soda water (optional)
	slice of lime, to garnish

Chill your cocktail glass with ice water or by sticking it in the freezer. Pour the gin, shochu and yuzu-koshō syrup into a cocktail shaker or jar with ice. Stir or shake for a minute or so. Strain into the chilled glass. Top with a splash of soda (if using) and garnish with a slice of lime.

Satsuma Sour
さつまサワー

What we call satsumas in the UK and US are actually *mikan* in Japan. The name comes from the old Satsuma domain (present-day Kagoshima prefecture), where they're typically grown. But the Satsuma name is actually more associated with sweet potatoes in Japan; in fact, the word for sweet potato is *satsuma-imo*. It's all a little confusing, but the double meaning served as the inspiration for this drink, which matches the citrus satsuma with the potato satsuma (in the form of shochu).

The measurements here are how I like it—quite sour, but not so much that it's a chore to drink or causes indigestion. Feel free to adjust the recipe to your taste.

Yield:	Ingredients:
about 2 cups (450ml)	3¼ tbsp (50ml) shochu
	juice of ½ lemon
	juice of ½ lime
	juice of 1 satsuma, mandarin or clementine—reserve 1 segment to garnish
	2 tbsp (30ml) simple syrup (1 tbsp sugar dissolved into 1 tbsp hot water, cooled)
	ice cubes, to serve
	fresh pitted cherry, to garnish (optional)

Combine the shochu, citrus juices, simple syrup and a little ice in a cocktail shaker or jar. Seal and shake until everything is really cold. Strain into a large glass and add ice. Top with a cherry, if you want, and the orange segment.

Chu-hi
チューハイ

(Shochu Highball)

The most ubiquitous izakaya cocktail is the shochu highball, or chu-hi, as it is commonly known. This is simply a measure of shochu topped up with soda, usually flavored with lemon juice and/or a fruit cordial. They are really, really fun, and I have a great fondness for them—I used to buy them in cans from convenience stores and smuggle them into karaoke booths, or quaff them at izakaya if I wasn't in the mood for lame lager. They're a bit like fizzy alcopops, to be honest, but far drier and more grown-up than something like Mike's Hard Lemonade and Smirnoff Ice.

The most basic and classic chu-hi doesn't use any flavorings; it's just shochu, lemon juice and sparkling water. But we can do a little better than that, can't we? The cordial recipes that follow are designed to go with the seasons, though most of them work nicely in chu-hi all year round. And because chu-hi can take almost any flavor, I've gone wild with my offerings. But if you just can't be bothered, you can make chu-hi out of pretty much any old cordial or sweetened fruit juice you have on hand. If you can get ramune, the Japanese soft drink, that's a real treat, as well.

The basic chu-hi recipe is as follows, but of course you should adjust it to be sweeter/drier or stronger/weaker according to your own taste. If you don't have shochu to hand, rum or vodka makes an adequate substitute.

Yield:
makes 1 drink

Ingredients:
3¼ tbsp (50ml) shochu
2½–3¼ tbsp (40–50ml) cordial (pages 236–237)
⅝–⅞ cup (150–200ml) sparkling water
ice cubes, to serve
slice of lemon, to garnish

Combine the shochu, cordial and sparkling water in a pitcher or jar. Swirl or stir gently to mix without knocking the bubbles out. Fill a long glass with ice and top with the highball mixture. Garnish with a slice of lemon.

White Peach Cordial
白桃シロップ

One of my all-time favorite fruits, exuberantly sweet and sexy white peaches are all the more precious for being available only one to two months each year. Enjoy this cordial in chu-hi while you can.

Yield:
about 1⅔ cups (400ml)

Ingredients:
4 large white peaches, pitted and chopped
water (see instructions)
sugar (see instructions)
3 tbsp lime juice, plus more to taste

Weigh the peach flesh and combine in a saucepan with an equal measure of water and half that amount of sugar, along with the lime juice. Boil until the peach is completely falling apart, then pass through a fine sieve set over a pitcher. Leave to cool, then chill and add more lime juice to taste.

Grapefruit and Honey Cordial
蜂蜜グレープフルーツシロップ

One for all seasons, but I think it's especially nice during winter in a chu-hi for the common cold.

Yield:
about 2¼ cups (500ml)

Ingredients:
4 large grapefruit
2 tbsp lemon juice
1⅛ cups (300g) honey

Zest and juice the grapefruit. Put the lemon juice and honey in a saucepan over medium heat. Add the grapefruit juice and zest, stir and bring the mixture to the boil. Remove from the heat and leave to cool. Strain the cordial through a fine sieve set over a pitcher.

Apple Cinnamon Cordial

アップルシナモンシロップ

This chu-hi cordial was inspired by a massive haul of sharp, slightly tannic fruit from my in-laws' backyard apple tree. Use green and sour apples, like Granny Smith apples.

Yield:
about 2 cups (450ml)

Ingredients:
3 green apples (about 10½ oz [300g]), peeled, cored and chopped
¾ cup (150g) superfine sugar
1¼ cups (300ml) water
1 tbsp cider vinegar
1–2 large cinnamon sticks (about 6 inches [15cm] in total length)

Purée the apples, sugar, water and vinegar in a blender until very smooth. Pour half this mixture into a saucepan, add the cinnamon sticks, bring to the boil and reduce by half. Combine with the remaining purée and leave to cool. Pass through a fine sieve set over a pitcher or jar.

Rhubarb and Custard Cordial

ルバーブカスタードシロップ

Rhubarb is no stranger to cocktails these days, and I've countered its tang with the flavor of a good custard: vanilla (not actual custard—that would be gross). Use this cordial to make a very British chu-hi indeed.

Yield:
about 2¼ cups (500ml)

Ingredients:
4 stalks rhubarb, roughly chopped
1 cup (200g) superfine sugar
juice of 1 lemon, or more to taste
2 vanilla pods, split down the middle with their seeds scraped out and reserved, or 1 tbsp vanilla extract

Place everything except the vanilla seeds in a saucepan and cover with water. Bring to the boil, stir, remove from the heat, cover and leave to steep for a few hours. Strain the mixture through a fine sieve set over a pitcher or bowl to catch the juice (you can use the rhubarb pulp to make a jam or sweet-and-sour sauce), then strain the juice again through a clean cloth or paper towels. Add the vanilla seeds and store in the refrigerator in a sterilized jar or bottle. Shake before using.

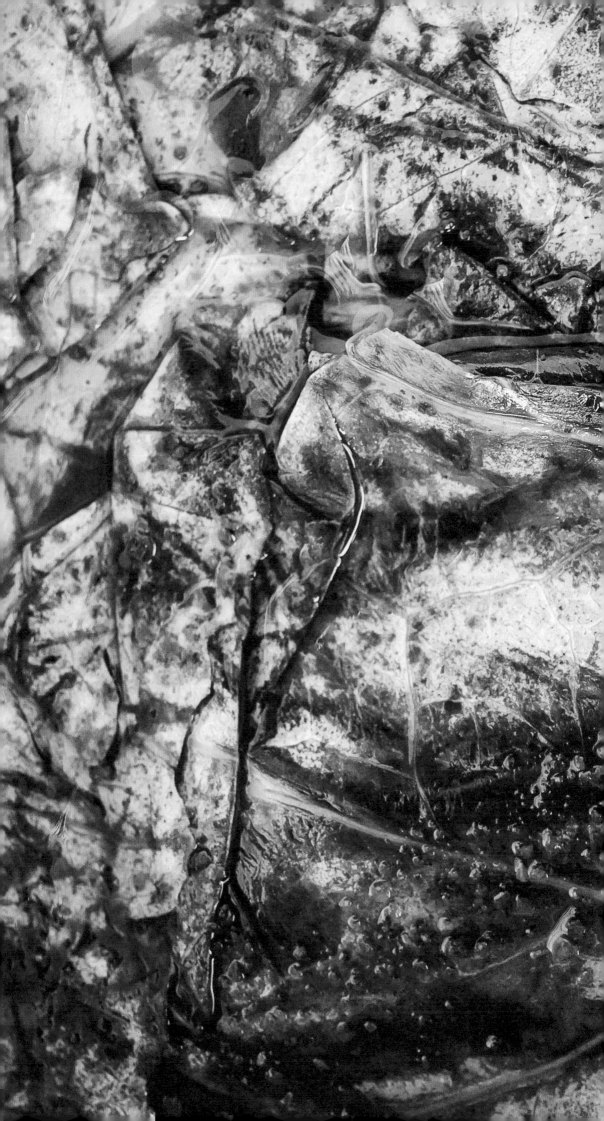

Useful Information

後書き

How to Eat in Japan
A Sort of Travel Guide

Ask the right question

The first question you should ask yourself (and answer) when you're planning a vacation in Japan is what do you want to get out of this trip? Do you want to indulge in Saga's unique seafood, the refined gastronomy of Oita's hot spring resorts or the street stalls of Fukuoka? A little of everything? Do you want to experience the "greatest hits" of Japan, or enjoy some of the country's lesser known destinations and dishes? Do you want to cover a broad geographic spread, or are you happy to stay in one or two locations? Answer questions like these and then get to work. One of the most common questions I'm asked is "I'm going to Japan; what/where should I eat?"

It's a tricky one to answer. Giving specifics can be perilous; if I recommend a restaurant, there will be a chance that it's closed down, that it's not good any more, or that my fondness for it had more to do with specific contexts than the food itself. If I recommend a dish, there's the chance that whoever's asking might try a poor version of it, or that they simply won't like it. Even among people who like Japanese food, I admit that my tastes can be a little strange.

So I think maybe the question itself is problematic. A better one might be "I'm going to Japan; *how should I eat?*" I can give specific recommendations, but that would impose unnecessary limitations on a country full of great food that's best approached with an exploratory mind-set. Instead, I think it's better to give general guidelines for making the most of your trip. So here are a few general dos and don'ts to keep in mind.

Do research and plan ahead

Find out about local foods; trawl the Internet, ask a travel agent or leaf through this book. You can either plan your trip around them (like I do) or decide on an itinerary first and then see what each of your destinations is known for. Either way you'll have great food. In most towns you'll be able to find the local specialties without much effort, but I'd recommend deciding on a specific restaurant or two and printing out maps to find them, because Japanese addresses are useless nonsense if you're not accustomed to them (and even then, they're pretty screwy). And that goes for everything, not just restaurants. Mobile data is expensive in Japan, networks are patchy and Wi-Fi is rare—you won't be able to rely on Google Maps when you're out and about.

Keep seasonal produce in mind, and try to eat a lot of it—like white peaches in summer, *matsutake* mushrooms in autumn, citrus fruits in winter and fiddlehead ferns in spring. Memorize the names of foods and drinks you want to try. Remember what they look like so you can identify them on menus and signs. Print out train and bus routes and timetables if you're dining out beyond city centers. Double-check restaurant opening hours—they often close on odd days of the week. It is totally possible to have a good time and eat good food if you just wing it, but it's more likely to happen if you make a plan. Save spontaneity for after dinner (and then go nuts).

Ask locals for help

English is not commonly spoken in Japan. It's not like going to Paris or Amsterdam. That said, most people will still be more than willing to help the best they can, using a combination of piecemeal English, gestures and maps or pictures. Hotel concierges, station attendants, shop workers and police officers have all helped me out with directions or with recommendations for good restaurants or bars when I didn't know where to go. And on more than one occasion, I've been offered help without even asking when I looked obviously lost and confused. People are nice.

Be polite

It goes without saying that you should also be nice. But I've seen a lot of foreigners in Japan act like entitled, obnoxious assholes. Nobody will expect you to know all the rules of Japanese etiquette, but a little decorum will make things more pleasant for both you and your hosts. You'll have a better time if you smile apologetically a lot and learn to say *arigato* and *sumimasen*.

Carry cash

And lots of it. In general, eating out in Japan is not cheap, and it's less common for restaurants to accept credit cards than it is in Europe or America. Furthermore, almost all Japanese ATMs have set operating hours, and you won't be able to get cash out after a certain time, depending on the day of the week. So be prepared. I forgot this rule one night during my most recent trip, and I had to run around for an hour (no exaggeration) looking for an open ATM so I could pay our bill. Not fun.

Stay in a ryokan at least once

Shacking up in a *ryokan*, the traditional inns of Japan, which are found all over the country in both cities and the countryside, is a great and easy way to try a wide variety of foods. Typically a ryokan stay is inclusive of dinner and breakfast, both of which are often memorably impressive multicourse feasts of local foods prepared by traditional methods. Last time I was in Japan I had two such dinners; one of them included delicious mountain vegetables and sashimi of a certain fish I'd never had before and probably will never get to have again; the other included around 30 immaculately presented individual dishes, all delightful and unique. A feast like this, accompanied by sake and followed by a dip in a hot spring and then bed, is one of the most deliriously relaxing and satisfying experiences you can have, not only in Japan but in the whole world. The hot spring resort areas of Oita, rural Kumamoto and Kagoshima are particularly lovely.

Slurp some noodles

Soba, udon, ramen, etc.—they're all good, and pretty much everywhere in Japan has its own special variation on at least one of them, like garlic ramen in Kumamoto, chanpon in Nagasaki or Shikoku's famous Sanuki udon. And learn to slurp. The way to eat noodles—especially ramen—is by aggressively hoovering in mouthfuls of noodles, guided through your chopsticks. This helps you inhale a good amount of soup along with the noodles while simultaneously drawing in cool air to prevent scalding your mouth. Once you get the hang of it, it's great fun.

Buy souvenirs

In most countries, souvenir stands are the last place you'd look for good food. Not so in Japan, where a culture of ritual gift-giving has given rise to an amazing array of confections, snacks and spirits available in train stations and hotel lobbies. The word for souvenir, *omiyage*, is written using kanji characters that literally mean "produce from the earth" or, in other words, "stuff from around here." Instead of generic cookies like you'd find at airports, you get treats made with celebrated local ingredients like chicken in Miyazaki, sweet potatoes in Kagoshima or crab in Saga. The majority of these are only sold in the place where they're made, so not buying them when you have the chance is a missed opportunity, and they're an easy way to get a quick taste of an area, even if you're just passing through.

Visit (super)markets

This is an obvious tip for finding good food just about anywhere, and it holds true in Japan as well. Tsukiji in Tokyo and Nishiki in Kyoto are two of the markets most frequented by tourists, but this doesn't make them any less impressive. Even if you don't buy anything, they're great for taking in the sights and smells. Be sure to visit supermarkets and department stores' subterranean food halls too—the former are good for fruit, snacks and ingredients to bring home, and the latter offer beautiful pastries, good booze, high-quality picnic fodder and excellent, jaw-droppingly expensive fresh produce, including the legendary ¥10,000 ($80) cantaloupes you may have read about.

Go to a festival

Summer is the season for festivals in Japan, but if you do a little planning, you can usually work at least one into your itinerary, regardless of the time of year. And sometimes you may just happen upon one unexpectedly. Festivals are great for cheap, often unhealthy food suitable to an atmosphere of beer-fueled revelry: fried chicken, pancake-wrapped hot dogs, soft-serve ice cream, buttered potatoes and squid on a stick are some of my favorites.

Don't avoid "convenience food"

Some of Japan's tastiest treats come from fast-food chains, train station kiosks, vending machines and convenience stores. In particular, *ekiben*—station bento—should be at the top of your must-eat list. Often featuring miniaturized versions of local dishes, these lunch boxes are one of the most enjoyable things about domestic travel in Japan. I fondly recall a bento from Kagoshima that contained small portions of 10 different local specialties, which allowed me a little taste of the things I didn't get to try during my stay, and a happy reprise of some of the things I'd already enjoyed.

Like train station fare, convenience store fare in Japan is entirely different from what you find in the UK and the US, partly due to the unique distribution model that allows multiple deliveries of fresh food throughout the day. The sandwiches, onigiri and salads very rarely sit on the shelf for more than 12 hours. They also boast more variety than you might expect, and are a good place to find cool KitKat bar flavors, like red wine or melon.

Don't dine sober

Local drinks taste good, a little Dutch courage makes you more open-minded to try strange foods, and with a drop of booze in you, you're more likely to ignore the language barrier and get to know some locals. A couple of premeal beers can often make the difference between a not-bad dining experience and one you'll remember with great fondness. (Too much, of course, and you won't remember much of anything. So be careful with the chu-hi!)

Don't skip breakfast

It's advice we should probably all heed even when we're not on vacation, but it's especially true when we are. Hotel breakfasts in Japan are usually surprisingly delicious and diverse, whether they're Western-style buffets or Japanese-style set meals. Miso soup in the morning is as invigorating as any cup of coffee.

Don't limit yourself

You don't have to eat Japanese food exclusively to eat well in Japan. In fact, considering it's a country where ethnic minorities make up less than 2% of the general population, the quality and diversity of non-Japanese food is often surprising. If an excess of rice or miso or soy sauce has you feeling fatigued, go get some pasta, French pastries or Korean barbecue.

But, of course, you should also always keep an open mind, even when it comes to things you've already had. When I first had mentaiko, the chili-cured cod roe famous in Fukuoka, I thought it was really quite weird. But after a few tries I came to love it. I know several people who've said they never liked sushi until they went to Japan, because it's just so much better there—if you cross sushi off your list because you think you don't like it, you may deny yourself a potential gastronomic revelation.

Don't be afraid

On my very first trip to Japan, back when I was a goofy and awkward 17-year-old, I spent an embarrassing amount of time in my hotel room watching anime because I was too overwhelmed by my surroundings. I still had a good time, and I more than made up for it on my research trip in 2005 and in the two years I lived there, but if you're only in Japan for a couple weeks, make the most of it! A friend of mine once said that Japan is the easiest place in the world to have fun. I'd say that's pretty true, but you have to let it happen. Go to arcades, go to strange bars, do karaoke, bathe naked with strangers and try as many foods as you can. You'll have fun and eat well as long as you are open to all the amazing experiences Japan has to offer.

Suppliers

Online Suppliers

E Food Depot
efooddepot.com
Offering a commendable selection of prepackaged food items and addressing all of your tea, instant noodle, and canned food needs, E Food Depot also has cookware essential for a Japanese kitchen.

Japan Super
japansuper.com
A family-owned business, this online retailer ships both fresh and frozen foods. They feature select cuts of Japanese style meats for sukiyaki, as well as fish roe for sushi.

Katagiri
katagiri.com
Established in 1907, Katagiri is the oldest Japanese grocery store in the country. It stocks a wide range of seasonings as well as tofu and natto. Delivery service is available in New York City and the store ships anywhere in the US.

Marukai eStore
marukaiestore.com
A one-stop shop for your favorite Japanese ingredients, Marukai even has a number of organic options. It also has a wide range of Japanese rice cookers and appliances.

Mitsuwa
mitsuwa.com
Mitsuwa ships items such as produce, meat, and fresh fish for next day delivery all over the country. You can also visit their bricks-and-mortar locations in California, Chicago and New Jersey.

Nijiya Market
nijiya.com
Nijiya Market ships Japanese pantry basics such as rice and nori, but do try to visit one of their locations (California, Hawaii and New York), where you will find fresh fish, cold sake and plenty of ready-to-eat meals.

In-store Only

Ebisuya Japanese Market
65 Riverside Avenue
Medford, MA 02155
781-391-0012
ebisuyamarket.com
If you find yourself near Boston, stop by this Medford, MA, store for restaurant-quality sushi and fresh pastries, as well as Japanese pantry staples.

Pacific Mercantile Company
1925 Lawrence Street
Denver, CO 80202

303-295-0293
pacificeastwest.com
This Asian food and gift store has been serving the Denver area since 1944. Today you can find everything from soup bases and seaweed to Japanese tea and sake sets.

Sasaya Japanese Market
1956 E Sunrise Boulevard
Fort Lauderdale, FL 33304
954-761-8010
sasayajapanese.com
Sasaya has all of your Japanese pantry needs, an extensive sake collection and a dine-in sushi bar.

Sunrise Mart
4 Stuyvesant Street, 2nd floor
New York, NY 10003
212-598-3040

494 Broome Street
New York, NY 10013
212-219-0033

12 East 41st Street
New York, NY 10017
646-380-9280
sunrisemart-ny.com
Sunrise Mart stocks Japanese staples and more, including meat, fish and a vast noodles selection, as well as prepared foods.

Uwajimaya
600 5th Avenue South
Seattle, WA 98104
206-624-6248

699 120th Avenue NE
Bellevue, WA 98005
425-747-9012

501 South Grady Way
Renton, WA 98057
425-277-1635

10500 SW Beaverton-Hillsdale Highway
Beaverton, OR 97005
503-643-4512
uwajimaya.com
Serving the US Northwest community since 1928, Uwajimaya now has four locations in Washington and Oregon, where you can find fresh produce, seafood and meat alongside a large assortment of Asian gift and grocery items.

Recommended Reading

The Book of Sake: A Connoisseur's Guide
Philip Harper
This concise but comprehensive book is an excellent introduction to the fascinating world of sake, if you'd like to delve deeper or find the perfect match for the food in this book.

Dashi and Umami: The Heart of Japanese Cuisine
Eat-Japan/Cross Media
An excellent Japanese cookbook covering many basic recipes as well as highly refined kaiseki dishes from four of Japan's top chefs. But what really makes it special is the appendices on the history and science of umami and how to best incorporate it into your food, Japanese or otherwise.

Izakaya: The Japanese Pub Cookbook
Mark Robinson
A compendium of simple, creative and delicious recipes from some of Tokyo's top izakaya.

Japanese Cooking: A Simple Art
Shizuo Tsuji
This is the Larousse Gastronomique of Japanese cookery, a massive tome that includes pretty much every classic preparation, plus an excellent guide to basics and helpful diagrams of key knife techniques and kitchen equipment. A wonderful resource for both novices and veterans of Japanese cuisine.

The Japanese Grill: From Classic Yakitori to Steak, Seafood, and Vegetables
Tadashi Ono and Harris Salat
If you like the grilled dishes in this book and want to learn more about them, or just want to host a full-on Japanese barbecue, this book covers a wide range of recipes and techniques.

Slurp! A Social and Culinary History of Ramen
Barak Kushner
Barak Kushner literally wrote the book on ramen, explicating its long and complex history from ancient China to modern Japan. It's a little expensive because it's from an academic press, but it's a must for any serious ramen geek.

Index

ACKNOWLEDGMENTS

Acknowledgments

This book could not have been made without the support and effort of a great many people.

First and foremost, I must thank my family. My parents, Mike and Nancy, and my brother, Benjamin, never failed to encourage (and bankroll) all my pursuits, however strange, throughout my entire life. I'm also extremely grateful to my wife, best friend and life partner, Laura, for sharing my love of Japanese food and for being a great cheerleader, an honest critic and an occasional therapist. So many times she has been like an oasis in the middle of a sandstorm.

More directly, I must thank my editors Rosemary Davidson and Rowan Yapp, Lisa Gooding and the entire team at Square Peg for all their hard work and advice. I feel like writing one's first cookbook shouldn't be quite as easy and painless as they made it seem. Lots and lots of love is also due to Paul Winch-Furness for making my humble cooking look beautiful. Many thanks, too, to my agent Rosemary Scoular and her assistants Wendy Millyard and Aoife Rice for making this particular dream a reality, as well as to my manager Holly Arnold for keeping the dream alive.

A number of people have fostered my passion for Japanese cuisine over the years, but most importantly, my undergraduate mentor Morgan Pitelka. He advised my many research projects on such absurd topics as curry and food museums, and helped me understand and appreciate Japanese food for all its complexity. This book is built on his teachings.

It would be an egregious error not to acknowledge the "MasterChef family" as well: Karen Ross, David Ambler, Vicki Howarth, Katie Atwood, Gregg Wallace, John Torode, Tony Crumpton and so many others. They made this book possible, not to mention my entire career as a chef. And thanks to my fellow finalists Tom Whitaker, Sara Danesin and Jackie Kearney for pushing me forward and sharing their knowledge to make me a better cook.

The London food scene in general has also been very supportive. So I must mention the following people who have been sources of inspiration, great collaborators and/or founts of wisdom: Fumio Tanga, Patrick Knill, Oisin Rogers, MiMi Aye, Emma Reynolds, Adam Layton, Lawrence Perera, Rebecca Song, Graham O'Brien and the Pressure Drop team, Mark Gevaux, Hugo Ushida, Uyen Luu, Rukmini Iyer, Rohit Chugh, Sarah Harding, Sujan Sarkar, Nikki Morgan, Ash Mair and Jon Dale.

Finally, many thanks to the people who don't fit in one category but have helped me in all sorts of ways over the years (they know what they did): Kylie Clark and the JNTO staff, Courtney Brigham, Emiko and Donald Pitman, Wai Wai Club, Kimura-sensei, Fujita-san, Justin Torres, Angeline Gragasin, Jordan Queen, Sarah Nahikian, Vijan Joshi, Amanda Lee, Luke Guttridge, Yuki Serikawa, Dylan Collins, Karen O'Donoghue, regulars and staff at the Euston Tap, Motoko Ezaki, Joel Harding, Stefanie Flaxman, Sam Schumacker, Dr. Barak Kushner, John Jones, Jay Rayner and the Kitchen Cabinet crew.

Kansha Itashimasu!

ABOUT THE AUTHOR

About the Author

Tim Anderson is a Wisconsin-born chef working in London. Interested in Japanese cuisine from an early age, Anderson went on to study Japanese food history in college, and then to live in Japan on a working vacation for two years. Since then he has moved to the UK to be with his wife, and he won *MasterChef* in 2011. He is now the proprietor and executive chef of the pop-up restaurant Nanban.

Photography copyright © 2015 by Paul Winch-Furness

Published in the United States by Clarkson
Potter/Publishers, an imprint of the Crown Publishing
Group, a division of Penguin Random House LLC,
New York.
www.crownpublishing.com
www.clarksonpotter.com

CLARKSON POTTER is a trademark and POTTER with
colophon is a registered trademark of Penguin Random
House LLC.

Library of Congress Cataloging-in-Publication Data

Names: Anderson, Tim (Chef), author.
Title: Nanban / Tim Anderson.
Description: First edition. | New York : Clarkson Potter,
    [2015] | Includes index. | Description based on print
    version record and CIP data provided by publisher;
    resource not viewed.
Identifiers: LCCN 2015045213 (print) | LCCN
    2015040765 (ebook) | ISBN 9780553459869
    (ebook) | ISBN 9780553459852 (hardcover)
Subjects: LCSH: Cooking, Japanese. | LCGFT: Cook-
    books.
Classification: LCC TX724.5.J3 (print) | LCC TX724.5.J3
    A73 2015 (ebook) | DDC 641.5952—dc23
LC record available at http://lccn.loc.gov/2015045213

ISBN 978-0-553-45985-2
eBook ISBN 978-0-553-45986-9

Printed in China

Book design by Charlotte Heal
Cover design by Charlotte Heal
Cover photography by Paul Winch-Furness

10 9 8 7 6 5 4 3 2 1

First Edition

Kyushu Libre Cocktail
Dark rum, potato shochu, yuzu-koshō syrup, cola

Hakata Gyoza • 博多餃子
Bite-size pan-fried pork dumplings

Trio of Kushiyaki • 串焼三類
...eef with hot mustard, chicken livers with umeboshi, and asparagus with bacon

Yaki-udon • 焼うどん
Udon stir-fried with bacon and many vegetables

...rashi Mentaiko Yaki-onigiri • 辛子明太子の焼きおにぎり
Griddled rice balls stuffed with spicy pollock roe

Mojiko Roll Cake • 門司港ロールケーキ
Black sesame sponge, banana miso custard, and fresh fruit

YOUNG & FOODISH
BURGER MONDAY
27 MAY

なんばん
NANBAN

Chicken N...
Chicken marinated in vin...
Crispy b...
Nanban tart...
Hispi cab...

"The Barbarian" w...
Pão doce...
Gochujang-Kewp...
Short rib/chuck/smok...
Mature Gouda and soy...
Shiitake, bacon, and 3...
Pickled o...
Katsu sc...

Go! Go! ...
Kinako cr...
Black and white ses...
Purple sweet p...
Hatchō miso...
Candied sweet pota...

OZONE
COFFEE ★★★
ROASTERS

ROTI CHAI
INDIAN STREET KITCHEN
& DINING ROOM

UMAMI-JI

なんばん
NANBAN
"Japanese Soul Food"

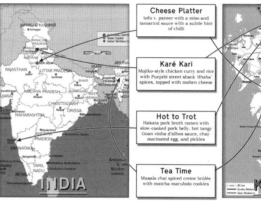

Cheese Platter
tofu v. paneer with a miso and tamarind sauce with a subtle hint of chilli

Karé Kari
Mojiko-style chicken curry and rice with Punjabi street shack 'dhaba' spices, topped with molten cheese

Hot to Trot
Hakata pork broth ramen with slow-cooked pork belly, hot tangy Goan vinha d'alhos sauce, chai-marinated egg, and pickles

Tea Time
Masala chai spiced creme brûlée with matcha marubolo cookies

INDIA

KYUSHU

なんばん
NANBAN
presents
"THE BARBARI...

An ode to foreign influences in southern Japa...
Featuring elements from the Netherlands, Portugal, Korea, J...
ONLY AT LONDON BURGER BASH • 7 & 8...

...祭 MATSURI
In London

featuring
TAKOYAKI • JAPANESE MUSIC
KARAAGE • JAPANESE FILM
SOFT CREAM • COCKTAILS
OKONOMIYAKI • BEER and more!

...ston Roof Park 20 & 21 July

THE RIB MAN and NANBAN
なんばん
KYUZU
HOT SAUCE
with Japanese Citrus!

南 全 鳥 蛮
Nanban
★ JAPANESE SOUL FOOD ★
presents
ZENTORI
at the Holborn Whippet
a 'beak-to-tail feathers' Japanese chicken lunch
Sunday, 27 April, 2014, 14:00–17:00

½ free range chicken + beer
Meal Deal!

Menu

Karaage 唐揚げ
Deep-fried chunks of chicken leg marinated in chilli, garlic, ginger, and yuzu

Chicken Nanban チキン南蛮
Chicken breast marinated in ginger and soy sauce, fried in a light batter and served with Japanese tartar sauce

Yakitori 焼き鳥
Grilled skewers of heart, liver, kidney, gizzard, oyster, comb, and parson's nose with a sweet-and-sour umeboshi glaze

Tori Senbei 鳥せんべい
Crispy chicken skin crackers with sansho salt

Chicken Miso Soup 鳥の味噌汁
Pulled chicken wing, neck, and back meat with tofu and wakame in a miso-chicken broth

Onigiri おにぎり

Slaw キャベツ

£25

PLUS! 1 half-pint each of
Pressure Drop Wu-Gang Chops the Tree and Pale Fire

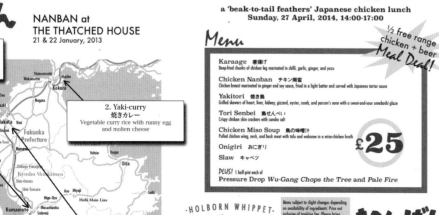

...ん
NANBAN at
THE THATCHED HOUSE
21 & 22 January, 2013

...iso

Shimonoseki
Wakamatsu
Moji
Kokura
Nogata
Hakata • Umi
Kata-Minami
Shin-Tosu
Fukuoka Prefecture
Saga
Chikugo-Funagoya
Yunhin
Beppu
Oita
Kyushu Shinkansen
Shin-Tamana
Higo-Ozu
Aso
Miyaji
Hohi Main Line
Kumamoto
Saiki
Kumamoto
Hisatsu
Yatsushiro

2. Yaki-curry
焼きカレー
Vegetable curry rice with runny egg and molten cheese

3. Mini Hakata Tonkotsu Ramen
ミニ博多風味とんこつラーメン
Pork broth ramen, chashu, marinated egg...

· HOLBORN WHIPPET ·

Menu subject to slight changes depending on availability of ingredient. Price not inclusive of booking fee. Please bring confirmation of your booking to the event. Tickets are non-refundable. Please note we may not be able to accommodate special dietary requirements.

なんばん

なんば...

NANBAN...
at STEPNEY CIT...

"Christmas in O...

17 and 18 Decem...